THE COLLECTIVE WISDOM OF HIGH-PERFORMING WOMEN

Leadership Lessons from
The Judy Project

BARLOW BOOKS
fine books for enterprising authors

Copyright © Colleen Moorehead, 2019

Foreword copyright © The Right Honourable Justin Trudeau,
Prime Minister of Canada, 2019

All rights reserved. No part of this publication may be reproduced, stored in a
retrieval system or transmitted, in any form or by any means, without prior written
consent of the publisher.

Note: The contributors have provided their business titles and, to the best of
our knowledge, they were accurate as of February 1, 2019.

Library and Archives Canada Cataloguing in Publication data available upon request.

ISBN 978-1-988025-38-4 (hardcover)

Printed in Canada
3 4 5 6

To Order in Canada:
  Georgetown Publications
  34 Armstrong Avenue, Georgetown, ON L7G 4R9

Publisher: Sarah Scott
Book producer: Tracy Bordian/At Large Editorial Services
Cover design: Ruth Dwight
Interior design and page layout: Ruth Dwight
Copy editor: Karen Alliston

For more information, visit **www.barlowbooks.com**

**BARLOW
BOOKS**

Barlow Book Publishing Inc.
96 Elm Avenue, Toronto, ON
Canada M4W 1P2

If you can see one, you can be one.

Contents

foreword

The Right Honourable Justin Trudeau, Prime Minister of Canada

Gender equality benefits all of us. When women have the opportunities they need to pursue their highest ambitions – and the resources and support to get there – they grow our economy, strengthen our communities, and blaze a trail for others to join them. And whether it's business or government or community leadership, we are better off when everyone, no matter their gender identity, has an equal hand in shaping our society.

Today, we're closer than ever to that reality – and the credit lies with generations of activists who have pushed for change, stood up for women's rights, and opened the door for women to access the highest opportunities. Thanks to their vision – and their tenacity – we've come a long way toward a gender-equal Canada. The stories in this collection are part of that history, and the leaders featured here are paying it forward, sharing their insight on rising in the business world as a woman. Being a leader means bringing out the leadership in others, and making sure there's not just a seat at the table, but a spot at the microphone, for those whose voices are all too often ignored. Because without that diversity of perspectives, expertise, and insight, we'll never move forward as fast or go as far.

Diversity has always been our strength as a country, and that knowledge has deeply shaped me on a personal level, influencing my roles as a leader, a dad, and a human being. Gender equality is a major piece of that, and anytime I get the chance to talk about it, I will, whether that's with international leaders, in a town hall with Canadians, or at home with my daughter and two sons. It's also been one of our top priorities as a government, and we took a strong stance from the start by naming a gender-balanced Cabinet – the first in Canada's history.

That unprecedented step has set the tone for our government and enriched both the policies we build and the way we do politics. From day one, we've brought a gender equality lens across our legislation, and that's driven groundbreaking progress – from introducing pay equity legislation, to creating a national strategy to prevent and eliminate gender-based violence, to supporting women entrepreneurs, to applying a gender equality lens to the federal budget for the first time. Canada is championing women's rights and gender equality on the world stage through our Feminist International Assistance Policy, and in 2018, we made gender equality the guiding theme of our G7 presidency, which led to a historic investment in education for the world's most vulnerable women and girls.

Measures like these are making a concrete difference in the lives of women and girls the world over – and growing the next generation of women leaders. But our work is not done. In Canada and around the world, we have a long way to go to make sure women and gender-diverse people have the same opportunities, the same support, and the same shot at success as men and boys. And that also means continuing to address the gaping disparities among women. Indigenous women, women of colour, trans women, queer women and non-binary folks, women with disabilities, migrant and refugee women, and others face unequal barriers – from a lack of opportunities and resources, to increased risk of violence, to discrimination and disrespect. To move forward together, we need to make sure the rights of the most vulnerable women are fully protected, and their voices fully heard.

Better is always possible – and the stories captured here hold wisdom and experiences that others can draw on in striving for change. Canada is making important strides toward a future where shared prosperity is a reality, and everyone has a real and fair chance to succeed. But to go the distance and stay the course, we need everyone's voice in these critical conversations that shape who we are, and who we're becoming. That means more women leaders need to be at the helm – in every sector and industry. And all of us can be part of making that a reality.

Introduction

Colleen Moorehead

Storytelling has long been used to pass wisdom forward from one generation to the next. And many of the storytellers are women ... with children by the fire, in their beds, on their mother's knee. This book is about storytelling. It's about paying collective wisdom forward from one generation of female business leaders to tomorrow's in order to sustain the societal change finally occurring in the workforce. It is written with optimism, and with the conviction that our future leaders — men and women — will value gender equality equally.

This is a leadership book full of stories by women who, during their careers, have truly lived the qualities of leadership that match their values. It's not meant to be "corporate speak" from a podium, but lessons learned about 10 values-based traits that truly matter. These crucial traits aren't textbook leadership qualities; rather, they reflect a more holistic concept of leadership: Courage, Honesty, Connection, Compassion, Energy, Lifelong Learning, Tenacity, Reinvention, Generosity, and Authenticity.

In these pages are the voices of women who have been part of a 16-year-old leadership program called The Judy Project. The program was named after a phenomenal business leader and friend of mine, Judy Elder, who died suddenly at age 47 of a blood disorder. She inspired many male and female colleagues; she was that rare sort of person who could create energy in a room. And she has inspired countless other people since, thanks to a powerful 2002 speech she gave about women and ambition. It went viral, and you'll see why when you read it.

I was there. That day, in that speech, Judy defined an inclusive kind of ambition — one that, instead of representing greed and self-promotion, reflected a broader, more noble approach: ambition for her company, her leaders, her team and, yes, as an outcome for herself. So compelling was her articulation of a generous, collective, female ambition that when she died three weeks after giving that speech, a number of us were inspired to create a leadership program named after her, lest this new definition of collective ambition be forgotten.

Why was this vision of leadership so compelling? Because it contrasted so vividly with the heroic model of leadership: command and control. When I joined the investment industry in 1983, I was handed a book titled *Dress for Success* and directed to Harry Rosen's for Women to buy three grey, black, or navy tailored suits. Like so many other women, I strapped on my combat uniform and joined a corporate culture that required women to adopt *male* characteristics, mannerisms, behaviours, and leadership styles if we wanted to succeed. We were told we were "too soft." Our feedback in performance reviews was consistent. "Be aggressive! Be more assertive! Be tough!"

But this culture collided with women's personal realities and socialization. We were arriving at the office after a total of three hours of sleep, with baby spit-up on our left shoulder and a to-do list that included dentist appointments, grocery shopping, and our children's science projects. Although we women had no choice but to bring our whole self to the workplace, the only part of us accepted in the corporate leadership world was a traditional male business façade. Attempting to compartmentalize our divergent lives created such personal discord that many talented women were forced to walk away. They could not be honest or authentic leaders.

"Command and control" policies had been in place in many companies since the 1950s, when the men who ran those companies and created the policies had returned from World War II. This leadership style changed very little after women entered the workforce in the 70s: you were forced to make work the priority, and figure out how to accommodate the rest of your life around that. I was once offered a promotion that would involve moving from Ontario to Alberta; I said "Yes!" immediately, because I had to seem keen for the opportunity. Then I realized I hadn't even asked my life partner what he thought. That's how visceral the desire to succeed was whenever we had the sniff of an opportunity. It was a Pavlovian response.

Fortunately, an awakening was beginning. Company women's committees became more prevalent. I vividly recall our small group of 16 or so senior women at CIBC in the early 1990s huddling together for warmth and survival as an HR consultant provided us with sensitivity training. She referenced the behaviour of our male colleagues as having originated from hunting meat as cavemen. This wasn't exactly comforting, and it's a concept we understand today as unconscious bias — something that has had a profound impact on the corporate world.

Over the next few years, the photo we had taken of our women's committee came to tell the story of our working-life reality. One by one, a black X was marked over each of us as we left the frame: extinction through attrition. I myself became an X, leaving the bank in my eighth month of pregnancy, a casualty of another corporate reorganization.

My silver lining was my corporate rebirth thanks to a mid-1990s financial technology company called E★TRADE Canada, where the business culture was less prescribed. As with Judy's experience, we were allowed to define a culture where celebrating our collective ambition allowed leadership traits such as empathy, generosity, and courage to surface.

★ ★ ★

The stories shared by over 70 women who have experienced The Judy Project are grouped in chapters about those 10 traits I mentioned above. These are widely recognized today as leadership characteristics that make our modern organizations stronger. When The Judy Project began, these were "female flaws" identified as weaknesses. The predominantly male corporate unconscious bias dismissed these emotion-based leadership skills, instead valuing the male-based skills predicated on toughness. It wasn't really their fault; it was how they were socialized. "Boys don't cry." "Keep a stiff upper lip." They simply transferred their unconscious biases to the workplace. But corporate culture has since evolved to embrace leadership attributes that match what millennials desire if they're going to maintain themselves in the workforce.

Each year, the new cohort of some 30 Judy Project attendees introduce themselves to the women who will become part of the balance of their successful business career. They are asked to talk about one of their role models. Although these role models vary widely, from Margaret Thatcher and Golda Meir to recognizable corporate leaders, a solid 30 percent of attendees consistently identify their mother as the leader they most admire.

These women describe the collective attributes of motherhood as courage, generosity, selflessness, and unrelenting support and ambition for their children. Those traits are *our* unconscious biases. And that idea takes me full circle to what's at the heart of this book. My mother had aspirations for me. And yours always wanted the best for you. But she didn't necessarily have the opportunities you do. So she made selfless choices.

The stories in this book reflect what your mother would have advised if the framework were in place for her to succeed. This is the collective wisdom of 16 years of Judy Project alumnae, captured by 10 leadership characteristics. It's storytelling learned from our mothers — and paid forward.

Through this book, we want women with aspirations of leadership to see that many successful women have had the same feelings you may be having — perhaps some sense of inadequacy, or a lack of confidence to talk about things that are gender oriented, like "Is it okay to say I'm planning to have a baby in two years?"

Those who follow the old autocratic leadership style don't collect wisdom. They don't stop to listen. So they don't benefit from what others think. But in new kinds of organizations — the ones in which leaders collect wisdom from others as a rain barrel gathers drops of water — everyone benefits.

Will this new way forward stick? Nothing is certain. But I think it has a shot.

PART ONE
Ambition Redefined

When Judy Elder talked about ambition, she made it clear that she was ambitious not only for herself, but for others as well. Judy's style of ambition did not create winners and losers. She wasn't fixated on climbing the corporate ladder for personal glory. She thought she'd win if everyone in the organization succeeded, and she was determined to make that happen.

In March 2002, when Judy was a senior executive at Microsoft Canada, she spoke about ambition to an audience of other aspiring women leaders as part of the Women's Television Network's Gift of Wisdom series. That groundbreaking speech, delivered three weeks before her death, created a legacy for female leaders. Here is an excerpt. (For the speech in its entirety, turn to page 219 at the end of the book.)

> I want to talk about ambition. Freely, frankly, and
> nonjudgmentally. Which is not often the way
> ambition is thought about when used adjectivally with
> women. Somehow "ambitious" is right up there with
> "aggressive" when it comes to linkage with the B-word.

As I've thought more about women and their ambition, I've come to the conclusion that, in our society's eyes, there are two sorts of ambition. First, and most applauded, is the desire for personal best — in sports, the arts, science, the professions.

But when it comes to organizational ambition, the passionate desire to lead complex organizations in business, government, and the public sector, we do far worse. We hold only 3 percent of clout titles — Chief Executive something titles.

Why is this so? Why are we celebrated for personal best but, dare I say it, blocked from organizational top-dog positions? Maybe because while women may be personally trusted, they are *less trusted to lead us*. We don't have *alpha people*, we have *alpha males*. When it comes down to picking someone who is going to win for us, we are inclined to pick the big strong competitive, undistracted, *yes*, ruthless guy.

And this brings me to one of the best pieces of advice I was ever given. An early boss and longtime mentor told me once that "people never get anywhere unless someone wants them to." Translation: Organizational ambition requires that others be ambitious for you.

Organizations are political. People quite naturally operate on the "what's in it for me?" factor: enlightened self-interest. If they are ambitious for you it will be because they believe in your ability to help them achieve their goals. When people are prepared to go on dangerous missions with you, you know they're ambitious for you because they see you as helping them win. Think of all the jerks who get ahead organizationally (the Enron leadership comes to mind). The reason they do so is because they bring others along with them.

I happen to believe that if you win for others along with yourself you will be rewarded with ongoing support and loyalty, and that loyalty will transfer from organization to organization, whether by reputation or, the truly to be cherished, people willing to follow you to other places. And by the way, I don't believe you need to be a jerk to get ahead; in my experience, most jerks eventually get their comeuppance.

Frank Clegg

FORMER PRESIDENT OF MICROSOFT CANADA INC., CEO OF CANADIANS FOR SAFE TECHNOLOGY, AND JUDY ELDER'S BOSS AT THE TIME OF HER DEATH

Breathing Energy Into the Room

"Frank, are you still there?" my executive assistant in Toronto asked. It was 6 a.m. on the west coast when she called with the news. After a long pause, I finally replied. "Yes, I'm here. I'm just trying to process this." But my stomach had dropped out. I was struggling to absorb what had happened. My GM of the consumer group, Judy Elder, had died. She was only 47.

And I didn't even know she'd been ill. We'd had a talk three or four weeks back, when she was deciding whether to travel from Toronto to attend a big meeting at Microsoft headquarters in Redmond, Washington. She said she had something personal to attend to at home, but didn't give me any details. I still wonder if I should have asked her for more specifics about what the problem was. But as a manager, do you pry into someone's personal life? And I knew her well enough to know that she would seek input, and then make decisions herself. All I could tell her was, "You have to decide whether this meeting is more important than whatever the issue is."

It turns out she'd been sick for a long time. Nobody at work had a clue about it. She had a blood disease and required frequent transfusions in hospital just to keep herself going. And her time had suddenly run out. The big thing that hit me was what a big loss it was ... to the company, to the industry, to her team, to her network of colleagues and friends, and of course to her family, her boys.

Because Judy was one of the most special employees we ever had, and one of the best leaders. Some people are black holes: they suck all the energy out of you. Judy was the complete opposite. She injected energy into everything she did. Now, there's a fine balance between being that person who is annoyingly rosy — the cheerleaders who don't know how to turn it off — and that person who has credibility, and who can step back and take a breath. Judy had a real gift for energizing people appropriately and positively. Yet she wouldn't gloss over problems.

A great leader like Judy is excited to see people do great things. She celebrated people, and mentored and encouraged them. I always thought she probably got up each morning and wanted to see what good things she could make happen. You could tell that quality was truly genuine and came from her heart.

Here's an example of her generosity. There was one stage when I was completely distracted over a few days by a mini-crisis happening at work. Judy somehow intuited this, so when we had our regular monthly one-on-one meeting, in which we were supposed to talk about what was happening with her business, 90 percent of our time was spent on her helping me out with this issue. She knew I needed help, and she wanted to know what she could do. And not because I was her boss; she was that way with everyone.

Judy was intelligent and approachable, and one thing she kept saying was that there's always a solution, and that we need to create an environment where people can come forward with solutions. She wasn't way out in front pulling, nor behind pushing; she was marching right beside you. She got mud on her boots the same way you did, and she did that for people both senior and junior to her.

We had a rigorous mid-year review process, a check-in with head office to see how your line of business was doing so that the company could plan for the coming year. Judy not only had to do this for her own area, but I remember her taking the time to help someone who was struggling in *their* own area — on another team completely unrelated to her business area. I didn't ask her to do that, and neither did the person she helped. That was how generous she was.

Her peers had the idea to create the Judy Elder award after she passed. One year, it was awarded to a seasoned manager in Ottawa. He had won Manager of the Year, another award we gave out, before that. But he called me after he got the Judy Elder award and said that it was the most significant award he'd ever received in his life.

I came to Microsoft when Judy was already there, and she and I got to work together for only one and a half years. And you know, to this day I wish I'd been the one to have had the honour of hiring her.

Cheri Chevalier

WORLDWIDE SALES LEAD FOR MARKETING TECHNOLOGY,
MICROSOFT CORPORATION; WORKED UNDER JUDY ELDER
AT MICROSOFT CANADA

Inspiring Others

In the short time I had the honour and privilege of working with Judy, she had a tremendous impact on me. Very soon after she started at Microsoft, we had our first real one-on-one meeting. Judy's default assumption about me was that I had the potential to do great things. I think this was her belief about many of the people she met at Microsoft. She sat me down and told me that I hadn't yet realized my potential, that I should shoot for the stars and think big — really big — and that I was amazing.

This, to be honest, was dumbfounding for me. She barely knew me, yet she assumed the best. She'd seen something in me and wanted to pull it out. It felt as if she'd placed her hand on my back, so to speak, and was gently pushing me toward where she thought I could and should be.

Looking back, I realize how important Judy's encouragement was. You need someone with more experience to tell you what you do well and what you need to do better. You need someone to believe in you, help you see your talents, help you see all that is possible. Judy saw potential in me, and she gently fanned that ember before she passed away.

Judy has stayed with me from that moment on. It's almost as though she's a silent mentor, guiding me without words but fanning the flame she created through the memory of her confidence in me. I find I channel her often before big presentations. I lean into the vision she had for me. I push myself to see whether what she saw in me is really there. I feel her hand on my back.

And now I try to do the same for others. I try to push people beyond what they may expect of themselves and give them a vision for what could be possible and where they could go. I try to give others that same confident push forward so that I, too, can be the silent hand on their back. It has helped me be a better manager, and hopefully a better leader, too.

> "SHE SAT ME DOWN AND TOLD ME THAT I HADN'T YET REALIZED MY POTENTIAL, THAT I SHOULD SHOOT FOR THE STARS AND THINK BIG—REALLY BIG."
>
> —*Cheri Chevalier*

There's a lesson here on the importance of filling people with confidence by assuming their capability. When people lack confidence, they can get easily discouraged and down on themselves — and it's hard to get them to be their best and do their best work. A word of genuine encouragement can stop the spin of someone's self-doubt almost instantly. With it, you start to feel stronger, and you bring conviction and energy back to the table. And you start to do great things. Suddenly you have the energy to take on bigger challenges, which leads to further growth and then more opportunities. I've learned that the spiral up can move at the same, or even greater, velocity as the spiral down when this encouragement is absent. And it carries over into the rest of your life.

So I challenge the leaders reading this book to fan the flame of young talent. Paint for them a picture of the future. Be that hand on their back. Show them a path. Encourage them by building confidence. It is the fuel of success.

David Powell

DAVID POWELL AND JUDY ELDER WERE TOGETHER FOR 13 YEARS
BEFORE HER SUDDEN DEATH IN 2002

Partner, Mother, Sister, Leader

Judy was not embarrassed to say she was ambitious. It wasn't a boast; rather, she was unafraid to talk about ambition. For her it was simply the natural order of things. She was never satisfied with where she was, and she always wanted the next job up. She wanted to be in charge, and she was convinced she could do a fine job of it. She'd counsel other women to kickstart their ambition too, advising them: "Don't be afraid to set achievable, practical but not threatening goals, and to envision doing your boss's boss's job."

For Judy, ambition was just another word for motivation. Her notion of ambition, of motivation, was far-reaching. She was ambitious for herself; she was ambitious for her people; she was ambitious for her organization. For her, the three were inextricably linked.

She once told her sister Kathy that she learned early in her school years that a leader needs an effective team in order to succeed. "You may have a lead role in the play," she said, "but nothing happens without someone taking responsibility for lighting, set design and costumes."

Judy had no commerce degree, no MBA. She graduated with a degree in English literature after four years of partying. Like many university arts grads, she had no idea what she could do. Her first "real" job, after stints as a waitress and a cook, was in the marketing department of Armstrong Floor Tiles in Montreal. (She always joked, "I really started on the ground floor.") Then after a move to

Toronto, she joined ad agency Ogilvy & Mather—stumbling into a field that she loved and where she excelled. Her world really opened up. From the beginning, she took advantage of every training course going, not just marketing but management and media training as well. Soon, she was identified by mentors who gave her support and advice on how to grow. She learned firsthand the power of mentoring.

For Judy, ambition was a collective strength, not simply a personal drive. She knew that neither she nor her organization could succeed if her people did not succeed. She invested in their growth, and with a generosity of spirit took genuine pleasure in celebrating their successes. Their success was *her* success—she knew that instinctively.

I think Judy could be comfortable being that generous because she had so much confidence in herself; she rarely felt threatened by anyone. But she was no starry-eyed idealist. She experienced firsthand the special challenges thrown at women by large organizations, and was not willing to accept the role of passive victim. For example, when she was passed over for the Canadian leadership job of a multi-national advertising agency, she left, joined a client—and overnight became the agency's biggest customer.

Judy made a point of taking media training, and at Microsoft became a go-to person for journalists eager to understand the new wave of technology. While her goal was to promote the company, it also enhanced her own brand. So when the Women's Television Network invited Judy to give a Gift of Wisdom breakfast speech, she jumped at the opportunity. She had been looking to break into the large-audience speaking circuit, and this was just one tier below the big leagues in Canadian business speaking venues.

I wanted to attend but Judy asked me not to. She was nervous and she felt my being there would make her more anxious. So, sadly, I was not there to hear her deliver a speech that would reso-nate with women around the world for a very long time.

But what she did after the speech was one of those telling details that really described what Judy was like. She noticed a young woman hanging back as other people came forward to ask her questions in the cavernous room. About a half hour later, when everyone else had gone, the young woman stepped forward. She was a little emotional, and said to Judy, "Everything you have said about ambition is all well and good, but how do you handle it when you suffer from a chronic illness?"

Judy was taken aback, and thought, *How does this woman know? Has she seen me at the hospital or my doctor's office?* You see, for almost 25 years, Judy had been battling a rare and myste-rious blood disease, a progressive disease that ultimately took her from us.

At the time of her speech, when she was running three Microsoft businesses and chairing the Canadian Marketing Association, very few people knew that she was spending about two half-days a week in hospital, and receiving blood transfusions every three weeks. According to her doctors, the majority of people on full-time disability were less disabled than she was.

But quickly after the woman asked Judy the question about chronic illness, Judy realized she was actually talking about herself and not about Judy. I asked her at home later how she replied, and she told me, "I didn't tell her about my own illness. I passed on three things that I had worked out for myself: First, don't be afraid, or at least try not to be afraid, because fear undermines everything and immobilizes you. Second, be honest with yourself. Decide what really matters to you—and do it now, because there may not be a later. Finally, I told her that whatever you choose to do, do it well. Make your time worthwhile. Make a difference."

The day after the speech, Judy received an email from the global head of Microsoft's Sales, Marketing and Services Group in Redmond, Washington. It read: "Judy, you are one of a small group of outstanding people who are seen as the potential future leadership of Microsoft. Get ready. We have things planned for you."

She was very proud of that e-mail.

Three weeks later, Judy died. She was 47.

Hardly anyone outside of our family and circle of close friends knew of the years-long battle she'd waged with the blood disorder. It ought to have been debilitating, but Judy managed her personal and professional schedule around the times when her energy levels would sag and she'd require transfusions. There were occasions when it got to her, but she rarely let it show. She knew she probably wouldn't live a long life, so she did her best to live a full life. She succeeded magnificently.

At the time of her death, Judy was general manager for Microsoft Canada's consumer division. She led the company through the dot-com crash, dramatically increased its market share and turned it into a technology success story. Her commitment to surprising and delighting MSN.CA users every day led to the successful launch of MSN Money and MSN Shopping—two key channels within the portal. Judy also steered the direction of Microsoft's Home and Retail division, which involved the marketing of Microsoft's software and hardware tools designed for productivity and entertainment. She guided the launch of Xbox in Canada in 2001. That year, she and her Microsoft team were named by *Marketing* magazine as one of "Ten Marketers That Mattered."

Judy was able to balance her big working life and her family life. She was an ambitious gardener, and loved to cook well; family dinners were important to her. She had Ernie, her Queen Street butcher, on speed dial. Frequently she'd call him, place her order, drive by his shop and lower the passenger side window. Ernie would throw the package into the car, and a good family meal was on the table not long after. She affectionately called her two boys, Peter and Jack, "The Rabbit Brothers" (as in, "Peter Rabbit and Jack Rabbit"), and we would gather as often as possible to talk about our days.

★ ★ ★

Since Judy's death, I've been amazed by the number of people who've contacted me to describe how she influenced their lives—both professionally *and* personally—and how she helped them learn and grow.

The funny thing is, I don't believe she truly understood the impact that she had on so many people. Take Denis Piquette, a veteran in marketing and advertising. He worked with Judy for almost five years at Ogilvy & Mather. Three years after her death, he published "Remembering Judy" in *Strategy* magazine:

> I envied Judy's ability to talk tough with clients and demand respect. Whether it was one of her employees being chewed out at a meeting, or a creative director being disappointed by having his idea shot down in flames, she would hear us out, take a few deep breaths, pick up the phone and tell the client exactly how she felt about it. Right between the eyes.
>
> Nine times out of 10 the clients felt appreciative because of her concern and compassion. They didn't view this as anger or being obstinate, they sensed passion and commitment, especially if the debate dealt with fundamental communications or business strategies. Whenever I sat in on one of those frank discussions, I felt empowered and supported. Her

actions meant that I too would be permitted to speak my mind.

For every presentation that I have written since my departure 10 years ago, I still start by asking myself: "What would Judy think or do in this situation?" And as long as this process continues to work for me, I will still refer to old pitches that Judy and I worked on as templates for success.

In 2005, Judy received an incredible posthumous honour at the inaugural meeting of the Canadian Marketing Hall of Legends, which was established to enshrine the people, brands, and stories behind Canada's great marketing successes.

The first-ever 10 honourees were elected by their peers from more than 250 nominees. On an evening that honoured Guy Laliberté of Cirque du Soleil, Dave Nichol of President's Choice, Ron Joyce of Tim Hortons, Christine Magee of Sleep Country Canada, and Michael Budman and Don Green of Roots, Judy was named to the "Builder" category. The category was described as "charismatic leaders who have built and enhanced existing brands and in doing so increased the competitive nature of their respective organizations."

At the time, I was stunned. I told one of the organizers that Judy would have been "gobsmacked" (she liked that English word) to have been included in such distinguished company. The organizer looked at me and replied, "You wouldn't say that if you'd seen the number of votes she got."

Always motivated by the desire to succeed, Judy's approach to success was refreshing and appreciated by those around her. "The thing about ambition, for me anyway," she once said, "is that it's not about the destination, it's about the journey." Sadly, she will travel no further. But The Judy Project will ensure that the journey continues for many others.

> "SOME PEOPLE ARE BLACK HOLES: THEY SUCK ALL THE ENERGY OUT OF YOU. JUDY WAS THE COMPLETE OPPOSITE. SHE INJECTED ENERGY INTO EVERYTHING SHE DID."
>
> *—Frank Clegg*

PART TWO

Ten Characteristics of Great Leaders

When The Judy Project was launched in 2002, our mission was to strengthen company performance by helping women move into leadership positions. We felt strongly that if more women entered the C-suite, companies would be able to tap into different ideas and approaches that might protect them from the dangerous risks of tunnel vision and lead to better, more enduring decisions. What's more, we believed that companies could grow stronger if their leaders exhibited characteristics that tend to be identified as female — ones like compassion and authenticity.

It turns out that we were right in line with the latest management thinking on what leaders should be. The old-style leader, as we all know, was like a military hero. He issued orders and expected his staff to follow. But in today's digitally connected world, the heroic leader isn't as effective as he once was. We're living in complex and unstable times, when the threat to a business can emerge in a flash from a 23-year-old kid in his or her parents' basement. As The Judy Project's academic director Tiziana Casciaro wrote in *The Globe and Mail*,

Leadership is really about creating a context in which others are both willing and able to do the hard work required to innovate in the face of ever-changing business challenges.

The job of business leaders in these complex and unstable environments is to create the conditions for others to come up with new ideas, to push forward creative ways to think about business problems and to help lead others in collective endeavours. As Harvard's Linda Hill puts it in her new book *Collective Genius*, these leaders of innovation say their job "is to set the stage, not to perform on it."

Casciaro, who came to Toronto from the Harvard Business School, is now professor of Organizational Behaviour at the Rotman School of Management and holds the Jim Fisher Professorship in Leadership Development at the University of Toronto. She thinks this could be a good time to be a woman in business: "As the increasing speed and complexity of business moves the dial from individual leadership to collective genius, societal gender schemas lead people to perceive women as better suited than men to leadership challenges that require inclusiveness, broad engagement and collective learning."

In this new world, the qualities of leadership described in the pages that follow are those that will make organizations stronger. Companies will be stronger, for instance, if their leaders are honest and authentic and, through their example, encourage others to adopt the same behaviour. That's not just a good thing to do in life; it will create the bedrock of trust that's crucial for any organization that wants its people to give their all.

This, then, is a good time for women to be in the business world. Yes, we have to *lean in*, as Sheryl Sandberg, Facebook's COO, famously called it when she urged women to shed their corporate inhibitions, speak up, and ask for the big opportunity. But we also need to nurture the qualities of leadership that galvanize people — and it turns out that those qualities are the same ones we've been promoting at The Judy Project all along. It's inspiring to think that the characteristics we admire in a person are the same ones that can help entire organizations survive and prosper.

"ONE OF THE INHERENT QUALITIES OF TRUE LEADERS THAT NOBODY TALKS ABOUT IS GENEROSITY. IT'S CRITICAL IN LEADING OTHER PEOPLE. GREAT LEADERS SHARE THE PROBLEM, AND THEY SHARE THE OPPORTUNITIES. THEY COME TOGETHER AND WORK IN TEAMS TO FIGURE OUT HOW TO SOLVE SOMETHING. PEOPLE WHO LEAD DO SO WITH OTHERS; THEY SHARE EVERYTHING WITH THEM — INCLUDING, VERY IMPORTANTLY, THE CREDIT AT THE END. AND IT'S A VIRTUOUS CIRCLE, SINCE THE NEXT TIME AN OPPORTUNITY ARISES, THOSE SAME PEOPLE WILL WANT TO SIGN UP WITH YOU AGAIN."

—*Shelley Lazarus*

1

Courage

Courage is the defining quality of great leaders. It's about standing up for values by calling out wrongs. It can also mean standing up for yourself and for others. And it can involve rocking the boat, creating discomfort, or threatening the status quo.

Courage is one aspect of the traditional heroic leadership model that, as women leaders, we need to preserve. We're often accused of being less risk tolerant than men are; according to the evidence, we like to have more facts than men do before we make decisions. I see this playing out in women's career planning: when a plum job is posted, a man doesn't worry whether he has each of its qualifications, while a woman often won't apply unless she has them all!

Courage can also mean resolving to leave when you're passed over for a promotion. It's the courage to walk away because you don't see an opportunity for the next level of leadership in your organization. And as you'll read below, that's far from easy.

"VALUES ARE YOUR NORTH STAR; WHEN ALL ELSE FAILS, THEY WILL GUIDE YOU."

—*Jennifer Gillivan*

Beth Wilson

CEO, DENTONS CANADA

Competing for the Top Job

I was hiking solo on top of a mountain in Colorado in 2017 when I made a brave decision: to leave the company I'd been at for 26 years. I'd had a great career at KPMG Canada, starting straight out of university and progressing quickly through the ranks. In fact, for the past 11 years I'd held senior leadership roles. And I had all the ingredients I could ask for to be successful there: talent, work ethic, opportunity, support, sponsorship, and a desire to have an impact. Yet I knew that leaving my job — without even having another to go to — was absolutely the right thing for me.

Let me explain. Back in 2006, I attended The Judy Project. I'd just been appointed KPMG's chief human resources officer — my first leadership role. I was excited, scared, a little overwhelmed, and lonely in terms of finding a group of people I could be comfortable talking to about the challenges I was facing. So The Judy Project came at the right time because it awoke in me the courage to call my desire to have an impact something different: I learned it was okay for women to call it "ambition" — and to embrace it.

I returned to work ready to tackle each new challenge with renewed energy in order to learn and to stretch myself. During those years, as I learned and grew as a leader, I began to see in myself what other colleagues, and my CEO, had told me they saw: CEO potential. Don't get me wrong; I loved being an audit practitioner and a client service partner. But I was always drawn to other initiatives, such as the firm's committees and task forces, where I could make a broader difference. I came to realize that I wanted to contribute in a way that went beyond what I'd been doing. I wanted to lead from the top. I was intrigued by the opportunity to bring my vision to life and unleash the potential of our people in a talent-driven organization.

So over the next 10 years, I focused on building my portfolio of experiences and learning from each role I had. I was trying to become a more impactful leader. But it was in 2013, while on my three-month sabbatical — which the firm encourages for partners during their careers — that I was able to focus most intently on taking that next step and forming my vision. My family took the trip of a lifetime to the Galapagos and spent the summer at our cottage. Meanwhile, I journalled, read about leadership — including Simon Sinek's *Start with Why* and Clayton Christensen's *How Will You Measure Your Life?* — and thought about my mistakes, what I'd learned from them, and my strengths. It was useful to have the time to become more self-aware and take concrete actions to improve.

In 2016, the CEO succession process commenced. People don't talk about what it's like to get into this arena as a woman. I'm here to tell you: it's intense. It takes courage to compete for a CEO position against a group of talented peers, putting a vision out there with emotion and passion. I was the first woman at KPMG to do so, and was *almost* the first female CEO of a Big Four professional services firm in Canada.

Even though I could tick every box on the competency and experience checklists, I was scrutinized intensely as a female leader. I found I was being studied in painful detail — every person I promoted, every business decision I made, the way I spoke, dressed, and presented on stage. I heard conflicting criticisms: "She's too people oriented and she's too soft" versus "She's not consultative enough and too directive." Not authentic enough, not personal enough, not a good role model, works too hard, has had it too easy. And: She's too ambitious. Too perfect.

For example, I was told that my delivery in public speaking felt overly rehearsed and was being perceived as not truly authentic. My messaging and delivery is something I worked hard on because I wanted people to really hear my words, understand my vision, and experience me as a leader — calm, confident, and compelling. Instead, those things often got lost because people spent time debating whether I was too polished or perfect or not speaking from the heart. In fact, I was always authentic and passionate; plus, I thought about the detail and delivery in advance, and I practised. I wondered if anyone had ever told a man he was too good at public speaking. What I experienced reminds me of similar criticisms of Hillary Clinton during that time period.

Still, I pressed on, surprising myself to find out how deeply I could reach for the strength I needed to face the politics and ignore the criticisms, confident in my track record and passionate about my vision. With the support of my family the whole way, I gave it my all.

But on a Friday morning, after deliberations to choose the next CEO were finished, I got the phone call from the board chair. I hadn't been selected. I went home and had a good cry while my 18-year-old son hugged me.

I don't think the fact that I wasn't chosen was explicitly about being a woman, although I do believe that organizations still struggle with the different style of female leadership. (I find that women are more inclusive, collaborative, and consensus oriented. They're more people-centric, drawn to the power of talent, and are better at systems-type thinking.) It could have been a combination of factors: politics, or maybe my strategy didn't resonate with the board. Regardless, that's when I discovered I had even more courage than I imagined — courage for my final act, which would be to leave.

I booked a trip to Colorado that very day; I wanted to heal. My younger son was going there for Outward Bound, so I decided to fly down with him and stay solo in a resort. I wanted to follow my own rhythm and do whatever activities I felt like doing — which included lots of contemplation, spa treatments, and hiking. But I went solo also because I didn't want to worry about the impact that my being sad might have on those I was with.

> "THE JUDY PROJECT AWOKE IN ME THE COURAGE TO CALL MY DESIRE TO HAVE AN IMPACT SOMETHING DIFFERENT: I LEARNED IT WAS OKAY FOR WOMEN TO CALL IT "AMBITION" — AND TO EMBRACE IT."
>
> —*Beth Wilson*

So there I was on one of my mountain hikes when I came to the realization that there was something bigger for me to lead — that I had to leave the comfort of an organization I'd been part of for over a quarter century (and am still deeply loyal to) and leap into the abyss. I had only the faith that I'd discover my next opportunity in due course.

Later that year I became CEO of the Canadian region of the world's largest law firm, Dentons. I'm not a lawyer; it was a bold but strategic move by Dentons to go outside the firm for their next CEO and to target a non-lawyer: a change agent. For the record, I don't think my gender factored into the hiring decision one way or the other.

As I said goodbye to my female colleagues at KPMG, I felt it was important to share my courage and support, and to pass on my learnings. Here are the thoughts I left them with via email.

From: Beth Wilson
To: All my Female Partners
Subject: Goodbye and a Few Thoughts for Your Action

Many of you have had conversations with me in the last few months that had a big impact. So, as I depart, I feel compelled as a woman who loves KPMG and believes in your potential to send you some thoughts and include three small (maybe big) asks.

I reached for the top rung and failed. Yes, I just used the F-word and I am okay with that. Note that I did not say "I am a failure" but merely that "I failed," which is true.

My first ask is that you be comfortable with this as well. You should embrace that I tried, understand why I was not successful — explore it, pull it apart, and ask tough questions about it.

Because, if you don't explore it, you can't learn from it — the institution can't learn, the leaders can't learn, and most importantly, women can't learn.

Second, I ask of you, don't be afraid to reach really, really, really high. Don't be afraid to fail. If you don't reach (out of fear of failure), you will never know what could have been and the world won't have the benefit of your talented leadership at senior levels. I had a lot of boxes "checked" on the competency and experience checklist and I still didn't make it — that is all the more reason why you should push, and push hard.

Third, please help each other. You have to help each other. If you felt at all compelled "to do something" after my unsuccessful bid to become CEO, then make a commitment today to truly help one another.

So ... what does help look like? Well, something like the following is a great place to start:

- *Recognize, celebrate, and talk about each other's accomplishments and strengths using powerful business language. "She is a great operator." "She has a great eye for talent." "She is active in the market." "What a great business developer." "Makes tough decisions."*

- *Don't get sucked into rock chucking. There are enough people lined up criticizing all leaders (male or female). Don't throw rocks at one of your own. We women are as guilty as men for criticizing women and falling prey to our unconscious bias … "She is too soft," "too perfect, must not be authentic," "poor judgment on that last decision," "too people oriented," "not inclusive enough," "too inclusive," etc.*

- *Leverage your voice to ensure women are on every slate, leverage your position to advocate for them and influence the decisions — there continue to be inordinate, subtle challenges for female candidates for any leadership role, so you have to over-rotate to support them. That takes courage and a willingness to let your own personal brand come under fire.*

I am convinced that KPMG has a future female CEO in its midst today. I would love to see the firm make that a reality before I am too old to recognize the name! I hope you take up the challenge and make it happen.

I am leaving KPMG not because I failed to become CEO. I am leaving KPMG because I want to continue to grow as a leader, because my work is not done. And after a stint in industry, I will take my experiences and leadership into the boardrooms of Corporate Canada and work from that platform to help break more glass ceilings for women.

I wish each of you all the best in your personal and professional endeavours. I wish KPMG future success to thrive as the great organization it is meant to be.

Make me proud ... I will be watching with anticipation and cheering for all of you. I want to hear the stories of how you reached, failed, learned, pulled another woman along, reached again, and succeeded, so please keep in touch.

Forever a supporter and advocate for you,

Beth

GOOD ADVICE
Young Women, Listen Up!

Know that female leadership most often needs to encompass your whole life; if we want kids, we don't have the luxury of not considering our whole selves. So look at your job as a part of your holistic life rather than as something that happens in a silo or in conflict with what's going on at home.

Eventually you'll have to make thoughtful choices about how you're going to spend your time and who you're going to spend it with. Create a "histogram," with yourself in the centre, and place the people with whom you spend the most time closest to the centre. Then put those you spend the least time with farther away. Who gives you positive energy, and who drains you? Draw arrows toward you for the positive, and away from you for the negative. Then have the courage to stop spending time with people who aren't net positive. You'll be surprised at how much better you'll feel by pruning your personal garden.

Seek feedback that will make you stronger — and then have the courage to accept that feedback. Being coachable is the least talked about indicator of future success. It means that you're learning and adding and adapting.

Remember this: There's no one decision you'll make now that's going to have a catastrophic impact on your life. There's no "right" path; you simply take the one that's most appealing, and then you course-correct when needed. So try to discover what you genuinely enjoy doing — and sure, there's some stuff that goes along with it that you *don't* enjoy doing — but do it with people you enjoy spending time with and in an environment that feels healthy to you. If you do that, it's all going to be fine.

All the successes I've had were from taking big risks, and I was prepared to fail. If you're going to fail, make it the most gorgeous belly flop anyone has ever seen — in other words, just commit to doing whatever the thing is. One mistake won't ruin your career. It's about taking risks. And even those risks that don't pay off are stepping stones to the next great thing. When you *do* flop — and you won't find a leader or CEO who at some point wasn't fired or demoted — then it's all about the rebound. The measure of you can't be taken when the wind is at your back; it's what you do when it's in your face.

—Lorna Borenstein
Founder and CEO, Grokker

Nancy Vonk

CO-FOUNDER, SWIM

How to Ask for a Raise

One of my proudest Mom moments was when my daughter bravely asked for a higher number when she got the offer for her very first job. Rather than this translating to every woman's worst fear — "Oh, then we're not interested in you" — it meant getting $1000 over the offer. In my book, that's one small step for a woman, one giant leap for womankind. Because the stats show that from the start, women don't ask for more than what they're offered — yet a high percentage of men go for more. And when it's time to go for a raise, that behaviour difference can add up to millions left on the table over the course of a woman's career.

Here's the thing: *If you don't ask, you don't get.*

And by all means, you should ask for what you want. Women have been conditioned since childhood to value themselves less, and to see going for money they deserve as unseemly. It's literally too awkward to bear. So we don't. Which means that, far too often, *we* play a role in the pay gap.

Women tend to think business is a meritocracy. Do a great job and the raise will come. But life isn't fair. The person who puts up their hand for the raise they want, and makes the case for why they deserve it, will get more than you, the patient, nice girl. So here's what you do.

First, find out what the job is worth. Do your homework. If a coworker in the same role will tell you what they make, good. What do people make elsewhere? Talk to a recruiter, or several.

Now you know what the zone is. (Entrepreneur and TED celebrity Cindy Gallop's suggestion: "Ask for the highest figure you can say out loud without literally bursting out laughing.")

Go in with confidence. When you get in front of the boss, for god's sake, don't bring an apologetic mindset.

Tell a story grounded in your accomplishments. The boss doesn't know everything you've done — maybe not by a long shot. Women tend to quickly discard warm memories of glory in favour of fixating on mistakes. Go back through your records. Your highlights are the reason you deserve the dough. *You want more money because of what you've done and what you're going to do.* The raise meeting is always a good time to declare your goals.

Before the ask, ask for feedback. "How do you feel I'm doing in my role?" is a great question before you ask for the bigger number. Their reply can be confidence building. Or, if you hear you have some gaps to fill, that's valuable learning that could suggest it's not the right time to go for more money. Get clear on how you can improve instead.

Tell the boss what's in it for her or him. Your vision for hitting company goals, and your enthusiasm and ambition for the job, are compelling reasons for your boss to give you a "yes."

Leave the boss time to think about it — and close the loop. Rather than ending the conversation without establishing next steps, which can mean your ask goes to the dreaded back burner, suggest timing for a regroup. "Can we put time in the book to talk again in a week?"

Jennifer Gillivan

PRESIDENT AND CEO, IWK FOUNDATION

A Lesson in Courage from My Grandmother

Each morning when I entered the gates to the all-girls Catholic school run by nuns, I had an awful feeling in the pit of my stomach. At my school in Ireland, where I grew up, girls were often belittled, and hit with rulers and straps. Not every girl's experience was a bad one, but because I was a little bit different from the others — more creative, let's say — for me it was at best an unpleasant experience, and at worst a terrible one.

One morning when I was 11, a teacher decided to drag me out in front of the class. I don't remember why. She called me stupid, pointed out all the things wrong with me and my schoolwork, and made fun of my size, saying I was big (I was tall for my age, and at a very sensitive time in my life). It was humiliating. At the lunch break I walked home as usual. I sat at the kitchen table, sobbing and devastated, feeling as if my soul had been ripped out. I believed that it was somehow my fault, that I was indeed stupid and therefore didn't deserve to go back to school.

"**WITHOUT A CLEAR UNDERSTANDING OF YOUR VALUES AS AN INDIVIDUAL AND A LEADER, YOU WON'T BE ABLE TO MAKE THE RIGHT DECISIONS.**"

—Jennifer Gillivan

Then my grandmother Dolly, who lived across the road, dropped in to say hi, as she often did. When she heard what had happened she said, "I'll be back in 10 minutes." Neither my mother nor I knew what she was up to. Soon she appeared dressed in her best outfit: hat, gloves, and brooch — looking every inch like the Queen Mother. She said, "Right, let's go back to the school." I said, "I am never ever going back there." But Dolly won the argument. Picture me at almost five-foot-eleven being dragged up the hill to school by my grandmother, who was barely five feet tall.

Into the classroom we went, after Dolly politely invited the Head Nun to join the class and my teacher. I was truly mortified, and wanted to be anywhere but in that classroom as Dolly proceeded to ask the teacher and Head Nun about my work. She asked to see copies of what I'd done, and, looking over my work, she remarked loudly to the entire class how wonderful I was, what a great imagination I had, that I was a talented artist, and more. I was flabbergasted. Then, still with her put-on posh voice, Dolly turned to the Head Nun and teacher and berated them up one side and down the other, warning them that if they ever touched a hair on my head, said anything bad about me again, or chastised me in any way, she would be back and there would be hell to pay.

In that moment of awe for my grandmother, my champion, and seeing the faces of guilt and shame on the teachers, I realized that you can respectfully but sincerely challenge authority — especially if you're in the right. My school days didn't get much better, but what changed in that moment was *me*. I realized that they didn't have power over me, that what I thought about myself was far more important than what anyone else thought of me. That having courage to be true to yourself regardless of what people think, and to respectfully dissent, was okay. It helped me become a leader and find my voice, my inner confidence to pursue my ambition.

THE MOMENT

In that moment of awe for my grandmother,
my champion, and seeing the faces of guilt and
shame on the teachers, I realized that you can
respectfully but sincerely challenge authority —
especially if you're in the right.

This kind of courage was hugely important in a challenge I faced in 2015. I'm the CEO of the IWK Foundation, one of 13 Canadian children's hospital foundations out of the 170 that form a U.S.-based group in North America. It's a group that has brought local foundations countless telethons and other fundraising vehicles and donors. But in 2015, the group was presented with a very challenging contract that did not represent the values or the best interests of our foundation.

When the deadline came to sign this contract, 169 members out of the 170 signed it — many under protest — leaving my foundation as the only one not to sign. I knew it was the right call and it had my board's full support, but it was one of the hardest and bravest decisions I've had to make as a leader, because leaving the group meant a possible loss of $3 to $4 million, and we had no way to make up those funds.

But then an amazing thing happened. The president of this U.S. group entered into talks with me, and not only were we able to negotiate a new contract, but in 2017 we formed a new group owned by the Canadian foundations. This provides an incredible opportunity in the support of children's health care at both national and local levels. It's the result of teamwork among the Canadian foundations — and is a win–win for everyone.

Without a clear understanding of your values as an individual and a leader, and without the courage to stand by them, you won't be able to make the right decisions. Values are your north star; when all else fails, they will guide you.

LETTER TO MY DAUGHTER

Lisa Kimmel
President and CEO, Edelman Canada

Dear Chloe,

I wanted you to know that I've always cherished our mother–daughter conversations. Even though the topics have changed over the years, it's always been important for me to make our chats teaching moments. But now that you're almost 12, I also wanted to write down a few thoughts in a letter, so that you'll always have my words to help guide you on your journey.

Take risks and challenge yourself. Trying new things is the key to attaining confidence. Have the courage to be comfortable with getting uncomfortable. The more you try new things and realize what you can do, the more you'll gain the confidence to realize you can do even more.

Surround yourself with people who support you. It's important to have people around you who love you and believe in you — they'll help keep you going when times are tough. In your career, find both mentors and sponsors to help guide you. While mentors are there to offer advice and support, sponsors will speak up and advocate on your behalf, even when you're not in the room.

Know what you want — and then ask for it. When I was younger I had a point of view, but I wasn't always comfortable sharing it. Other people can be great role models, but you need to figure out what *you* want — and then ask for what you need to succeed. Establish your own boundaries, make deliberate choices, and don't let your life be imposed upon you.

Love,
Mom

Carol McNamara

SENIOR VICE PRESIDENT, COMPENSATION & BENEFITS, RBC

The Courage to Take Time Out for Family

Years ago, when my four children were all under the age of six and my husband was travelling frequently, I was fighting a losing battle in trying to be my best both at work and at home. Part of the problem was that we'd moved from Montreal to Toronto and had no family support network. So I decided to step out of the workforce for an indefinite period of time.

Up to that point I'd been fortunate to work in an environment that enabled me to take time away from my career as my children were born. I made compromises, in particular passing up some interesting work opportunities, but felt confident that I was making the right choice for our family, and that I could thus make a stronger contribution to my workplace each time I returned.

So my decision to step back was a tough one, and one I had to muster my courage to make, even though my husband — and closest confidant — was in my corner no matter what I decided. It was a period of real introspection, of holistically weighing the variables in an equation of career ambition, personal well-being, and confidence that I could resume my career at RBC, or elsewhere, when the time was right.

I figured I needed more than a year off, and I didn't think it was fair to the company to ask for any longer than a year, so I left with no formal path back in. I chose not to discuss this with my manager, and that's something I regret because, as a manager myself at this stage in my career, I encourage these conversations from women who are struggling to integrate work and family. Women need to be able to look up to senior levels in the organization and see leaders who've shared these career/family juggling experiences. It's just one way we can contribute to an inclusive workplace.

One of the toughest aspects was my guilt. I felt I was letting down my management team, even though they were forward thinking. Worse, by leaving I felt I might be letting other women down — particularly those coming along behind me who might also want flexible arrangements.

Still, I knew I was doing the right thing for me, and don't regret my decision. Being home enabled me to be more engaged and emotionally present in the moment. I was now able to manage all the school and preschool routines, and attend a mother-and-baby group. I enrolled the kids in after-school sports and music and dance classes, which would have been harder to coordinate had I been working. And my favourite times were the unstructured activities, such as exploring museums, art galleries, and the zoo, or just going to the playground.

But life is full of unanticipated turns. When a year of my leave had passed, my father, who lived in Calgary, was diagnosed with cancer. I spent at least a week out of every month with him there, helping to care for him. Each time I returned home I'd hit the ground running with my busy family routine.

After my father passed away, I was emotionally and physically exhausted. And I realized that, having been out of the workforce for a year and a half, I was missing my time at the office — something that was an investment in myself, and important to my sense of self-worth. Fortunately, I received a call from my former manager asking if I'd consider returning to RBC. I jumped at the chance, although I did ask for some flexibility in my work arrangement. I feel fortunate to be working for a company that was there with open arms when the time was right to return to work. And it was a win-win, because it served to deepen my loyalty to and engagement with RBC.

I often reflect on that period as the experience that instilled in me a long-term perspective on career. Career isn't necessarily linear — it can be a series of recalibrations of priorities. It took giving it up to realize that I was missing an important source of positive energy. And I learned through my experience that how one measures ambition and success is very personal.

Shelly Lazarus

CHAIRMAN EMERITUS, OGILVY & MATHER

Speaking Up for What's Right for You

I'd been a management supervisor at American Express for just three weeks (this was a big-deal job!) when an all-day meeting was scheduled to discuss the entire marketing strategy for the next five years. The meeting was to start at 8:30 a.m. I explained to my new client, who was the marketing head, that I wouldn't be able to get there until 1 p.m. because it was Field Day at my son's school. His response: "You're kidding, right?"

I assured him that I was most definitely not kidding, and explained that within the space of a week or two he wouldn't be able to recall who was actually at that strategy session, because 25 people had been invited. And, I reasoned, if one person wasn't there for a few hours, who would remember? On the other hand, I said, my eight-year-old would never forget that his mother hadn't come to his Field Day.

I knew where I had to be … I knew where I was *going* to be. If anyone didn't like it, they could fire me.

There is so much to do — but you can only do so much. And I'd argue that the lack of courage to speak up about what's right for you and for your family is perhaps the biggest obstacle we, as women, put in our own way. We all put on these game faces when we come to work. But it's not honest; it's isolating. And in the end it does us a disservice, and does a disservice to the companies we work for, because the greatest loss companies face is the loss of good talent due to a lack of understanding of real lives. It happens all the time.

Courage is essential for gaining balance in your life. You must have the courage to say, "This is what I need to do. This is what's important to me." You can't expect the people around you to understand or respect your priorities if you don't tell them … and act on them.

So I say, speak up. Be who you are. Live your values. I never snuck out to attend the school play or go to the pediatrician appointment; instead, I walked straight down the centre aisle. And the truth is that in 35 years, no one ever confronted me about it. I was never challenged. Not once. What's the worst thing that can happen? They fire you … Yeah, maybe. But probably not. Especially if you're good.

Here's my advice: First, become indispensable. Then tell them what you need.

"THE LACK OF COURAGE TO SPEAK UP ABOUT
WHAT'S RIGHT FOR YOU AND FOR YOUR FAMILY
IS PERHAPS THE BIGGEST OBSTACLE WE, AS
WOMEN, PUT IN OUR OWN WAY."

—*Shelly Lazarus*

GOOD ADVICE
Embrace Risk

I heard a brilliant speech by the actor John Cleese many years ago. He talked about organizations where the first priority is "not to fail" — those places where the watch words are "Whatever you do, don't make a mistake … just don't screw it up." In those places there will never be innovation — because innovation, by its very nature, is all about trying something that has never been tried before. In those organizations, you can't try anything new because the stakes are too high. This is lethal.

Not every decision has to be a life-or-death, winner-take-all situation. There's a middle way; it's called experimenting. Personally, I'm not happy unless I have a lot of pots on the stove ... things I'm trying out. Three-quarters of them may be wrong (courage!), but a quarter will be right. And if you don't have four brewing at all times, you won't have your next program, your next chapter ... your next success. So go for it.

It also helps if you "de-risk" your decisions. When a decision is in front of me, I get very focused on potential outcomes. I ask myself, "What's the worst thing that could happen?" Usually, the worst thing is that I could get fired. Okay, if you're talented and have self-confidence, let them fire you. You'll land on your feet.

But if you're talented, they won't fire you. Now you've de-risked the decision. Whatever consequence there is, you can handle it.

—Shelly Lazarus

2

Honesty

*E*veryone has faced that moment when you wonder whether you should say, "I don't like it when you talk to me like that." It's hard to muster the courage to plainly speak your truth. You're concerned about how your boss might react — whether he or she will be offended, whether there will be repercussions. But consider the consequences of staying silent. You're beginning to retreat; you're not acting authentically. At that moment, you don't even know if the other person is aware of the issue. When there is no honesty, there is no trust, and the environment changes. Everyone around you feels it.

> "I KNEW THIS WAS PRECISELY THE TIME TO BE GUIDED BY MY AUTHENTICITY AND LIFELONG INCLINATION, FOR BETTER OR WORSE, TO BE HONEST."
> —*Nancy Vonk*

Fostering a culture of honesty, the very foundation of trust, can have a deep and positive impact on productivity. People contribute the most in an environment of trust: they feel free to express their ideas, even if they're ultimately shot down. If trust is lacking because people aren't being honest with one another, you might withhold an idea, fearing rejection or derision. You can't contribute as a high performer, and neither will the team — and in a highly competitive world, that will undermine your organization's prospects for long-term success.

Nancy Vonk

CO-FOUNDER, SWIM

On Being a Truth Teller

"There are news trucks in front of your house!"

My neighbour's breathless phone call jolted me awake early in the morning of Wednesday, October 8, 2005. *This isn't happening.* A moment after stuttering my thanks to her, a producer from NBC News was on the line from New York. There would be many more calls that day from global media. From my CEO. From my worried sister in California. By late afternoon my friend and competitor Judy John, the creative leader of Leo Burnett in Toronto, would call from India saying, "Oh my god Nancy, are you okay?" I burst into tears.

Forty-eight hours earlier I'd been sitting in an audience at an advertising event called "An Evening with Neil French" — he was an industry guru and the revered CCO (chief creative officer) of my global network. I was the Toronto co-CCO then, and had looked forward to this night for months. Neil was my longtime leader, mentor, and friend. The talk was shot through with his signature sense of humour, but Neil's expression suddenly went dark after a young woman's question during the Q&A that followed. "Why aren't there more female creative directors?" In a voice dripping acid, he began rattling off a long list of reasons why women don't deserve the position. "They won't commit. I don't know why we even give them a chance — they'll just run off and suckle something." He mimed cradling a baby and shoved his arms toward his chest as he spat out those words. He framed women as slacker breeders who wouldn't put in the hours.

With front-row seats to the spectacle, my friend and co-CCO partner Janet Kestin and I exchanged horrified expressions. Next to her, Steve Hayden, our agency's top creative leader in the New York office, looked ill. He leaned over to whisper, "Oh my god." In these few surreal, devastating moments, my relationship with Neil imploded. Filing out afterward, I heard advertising students who'd travelled from Virginia to be there saying things like, "I guess I chose the wrong career." Women headed for the exit with ashen faces. I felt an urgency to *do* something. But what in hell was the right thing to do?

One thing I knew I must do was to confront Neil at the after party, something just hours earlier I'd expected to be the best part of the evening. I waited for him to arrive at the Westin hotel bar, my stomach a tight fist. As he ordered a drink beside me it was obvious he hadn't had the first thought about the topic that would very shortly prove life-altering for both of us. A deep breath, then: "Neil, you can probably imagine I have a problem with what you said about women." He was having none of it. After brief hellos with friends in the crowd, all avoiding talk of the elephant in the room, Janet and I left.

By the next day, I knew what I could do. Rather than leaving "women can't cut it" hanging in the air, this female leader and mother of Lily could declare otherwise. And I could do it on the advertising site ihaveanidea.org, where people had bought their tickets for the talk. The very site that had recently promoted *Pick*

Me: Breaking into Advertising and Staying There, a book I'd co-written with Janet that featured Neil on the cover as a star contributor.

From the heavy antique desk in my basement office I stared up through the window as falling leaves blew against the glass. I was getting nowhere. Doubts weighed in, and the words wouldn't come. What if I failed to tell the story clearly, or fairly? Would I be out of a job? Should I consult with mentors before challenging the global CCO?

The words finally started to flow as certainty kicked in. I knew this was precisely the time to be guided by my authenticity and lifelong inclination, for better or worse, to be honest. It was important to speak up for the sake of others — the students, all the women hitting brick walls, all the men who lead and work with women. I was focused and calm by the time I wound down with "For all the young people at the Neil French night, especially, I hope you will retain the many pearls of wisdom he had to share and use them to your benefit. This ad giant has many good lessons to teach. As for his perspective on women, consider it the perfect demonstration of one of the biggest obstacles to success women face and see it for what it really is: a load of crap that inspires you to prove Neil and friends wrong."

Janet was quick to support it and to contribute her editing skills. I told Ignacio Oreamuno, the young ihaveanidea.org founder, that the piece needed to be posted no matter the outcome. He didn't flinch.

My deeply critical pushback to Neil's words would be read by many more than the people in that Toronto theatre. It went viral. Shortly after news trucks appeared at my door, the blog post heard around the world had sparked headlines from London to Sydney. It was on the front pages of *The New York Times, The Globe and Mail,* in *Time* magazine and every international trade publication.

I did indeed take penalties, along with Janet, who'd gone on to write and speak publicly about the darker side of the industry response to the essay. The immediate fallout had included thousands of comments like "Come on girls, put your ovaries back in your uterus" and "Have you ever considered maybe you ARE a f-ing bitch?" "Get ready for sensitivity and diversity classes. The lights are going to go off earlier and earlier as women head home to the kids." Although there were many supportive posts, I stopped reading any of them after the first few days. It was painful if not surprising to become a pariah, overnight, to peers in the network I had known for years.

But in the long run, I saw reward for speaking my truth. Whereas I lost status with Friends of Neil, I gained it with a far larger group. This story was instantly perceived as evidence of a festering, chronic problem in all industries. The experience opened my mind to the harsh realities of gender bias in the workplace, bias that I'd been wilfully blind to for decades. It opened doors to meeting people who would deepen my education on the issue. With new-found passion for supporting women's success, I would find myself speaking at schools, organizations, and companies around the world. Janet and I would be named Women of the Year by New York and L.A. women's organizations. I was even commissioned by HarperCollins to write a career guide for women, *Darling, You Can't Do Both (And Other Noise to Ignore on Your Way Up)*. It led to a rewarding second career, grounded in my personal values. Janet and I co-founded Swim, our "creative leadership lab," in 2012.

The Neil saga has cemented my belief that the leader who makes authenticity and honesty her guide will find the greatest work and life success. Being willing to say what others won't, when it's for the sake of the group's success, is a winning long-game strategy and promotes sleeping well. In the painful heat of the moment, I was buoyed by Stan Sutter's *Marketing* magazine article, "Bringing Down the Bull Moose": "Nancy Vonk's response to comments [like Neil's] can't be a big surprise to anyone who knows her." And by my friend and former Ogilvy peer Joe Sciarrotta's words: "Well, Nancy, what else could you do? That was totally on brand." It would be okay. More than okay.

On October 21, 2005, after two weeks with his heels dug in, Neil resigned. I knew that day my obituary would lead with "The woman who brought down Neil French." In fact, he brought himself down, in charge of his own destiny. But what I wouldn't at all mind being best known for when time's up is as a truth teller; someone who believed there was much to be gained in work and life by putting honest words — hard words that needed to be shared — into every room I could.

Cheryl Brunato

VICE PRESIDENT, XPLORNET

Make Your Aspirations Known

I had an epiphany earlier in my career that changed my career path. A job opportunity came up that would have required a lot of travel — three to four days per week, for about a year. I was the best choice for this job given that I had the most relevant experience, and so I was hopeful I'd get it. Then I heard from others at work that my boss assumed I wouldn't want the opportunity. Why? Because I had a seven-year-old son. So I went to my boss and told him that I was interested. After our discussion I was given the role, and that position was a key step in my career path.

My takeaway was that you have to be honest and upfront, and not assume that others will be aware of your career aspirations. Communication rather than assumption — both on my part and my boss's — was the key in this situation. I learned that if I don't make my goals and interests known, how can I expect anyone else to know them?

> **"ACKNOWLEDGING THAT THERE *IS* NO BALANCE — ONLY WHAT COMES FROM CONTINUING TO STRIVE TOWARD YOUR FAMILY'S VERSION OF WORK–LIFE INTEGRATION — IS IMPORTANT TO FINDING YOUR HAPPINESS."**
>
> *—Kathleen Taylor*

I take the message of honesty and openness to my teams. Together, we establish guiding principles on how each team is going to work. The themes that consistently show up are collaboration and respect. Collaboration in particular is so important, as it allows people to engage in honest discussions that ultimately lead to the best solutions.

For example, not long ago I had a team looking to solve a future IT capacity problem. Everyone was going down the same path: a traditional solution at a very high cost. Then one team member spoke up and said, "What if we consider another option?"

He explained his idea for the IT systems design, and the team brainstormed its pros and cons. In the end, this new option was selected — and not only was the cost just 25 percent of the other solution's, it was a more robust design.

Thank goodness that team member felt he had an open forum to bring forward his idea. Without the guiding principles supporting open and honest discussions, great solutions might never come to light.

Kathleen Taylor

CHAIR, RBC

How to Integrate Your Work with Your Life

When I'm asked about my many years heading up Four Seasons Hotels and Resorts, one of the questions I get a lot is "What was the toughest decision you ever had to make?" The answer? It wasn't corporate in nature; it wasn't a life-and-death business decision about a big transaction or a new hotel. The decisions I struggled with most were around how to raise a young family, and to do that while frequently on airplanes and in different countries as part of my day job.

Based on my experience, the advice I share with young women today is honest and straightforward: There is no "all"; there's no such thing as "work–life balance." Instead, I say that it's about *your* all and how you find your own version of work–life integration. Women often see others and think, *If I could only have the balance she has, I'd be okay.* But in fact, there is no single recipe. I chose the one that worked for me and my family (more on that later). The circumstances of family raising are different for everyone. So don't benchmark yourself against someone you think has it all figured out, because the likelihood of that being true isn't very high.

We keep talking about how to attain balance. But acknowledging that there *is* no balance — only the appearance of balance that comes from continuing to strive toward your family's version of work–life integration — is important to finding your happiness. I always make the analogy of the tree pose in yoga. That balance pose is really hard when done well, and in fact it's not about achieving balance at all — it's actually about using strength to create the outward appearance of balance ... figuring out how you stay strong.

Decide with your partner how you'll raise your family. I travelled quite a lot for work, so my husband and I decided early on that he'd be the go-to parent for things like sports and school events. And we had tons of help from all sorts of different places: my parents took care of our kids when he and I both travelled, as did my sister and brothers, our nanny, and others.

Now the kids are grown up, and they love to talk about those days. They make good-natured fun about how I wasn't around as much as their dad. For example, one time when the kids were young I was really sick and was ordered by my doctor to rest. After a couple of days at home lying around I got bored, so I started baking cookies. One day I even went to pick my daughter up from school. In those weeks, I thought I might be the perfect version of myself.

But this me was so foreign to them. And they joked about it at a family gathering: "It was so creepy! She was in the kitchen every day when we got home! Then she showed up at school to pick me up like a stalker!" It was so beyond what they'd been expecting, and they certainly didn't like the change to their routine!

So just as you set expectations with your manager at work, you set expectations at home. For me and my husband, this was the recipe for a happy home life.

Be honest and open at work. In my early days at Four Seasons there were very few women at the executive level, so being a working mom was relatively new. Fortunately, my boss and his boss and our founder and CEO — all males — were very supportive of the idea of me just getting on with the business of doing my job and having a family. They all had children and were married to strong women, true partners in their lives. All that helped give me the latitude I needed to focus on my version of work–life integration.

I remember bringing my newborn daughter to the office with me when she was just four weeks old. This was mainly because our son was acting out at home due to the arrival of his new sister. She slept most of the time in a porta-crib in my office, allowing me to do what I loved all day — and yes, that was business — while keeping her close for feedings. That arrangement sounds insane to many, and there was no shortage of people who judged me even back then. But I made a choice that worked for our family, and that fortunately worked for my colleagues at Four Seasons as well.

Make daily conscious choices. Every day something presents itself that throws you out of alignment, challenging your most recent recipe for work–life integration. It can be anything — big or small — from your dog is sick, to your sister has broken her leg, to your child is facing a challenge of some sort. You need to be ready to adjust your priorities on pretty short notice.

The day I was appointed CEO of Four Seasons my mother passed away. She'd been suffering from Alzheimer's for some time, so her death wasn't a shock, but it did mean I had to change everything I'd planned to do in the coming days. Press interviews the next day, along with time with hotel partners, my senior team, and employees in the week following ... it all had to be rearranged to make room for the time I needed to spend with my 90-year-old father and my siblings.

That's a pretty dramatic example for sure, but it's a reminder nonetheless that every day you have to take stock of what's changed since yesterday — and then adjust so that you're making wise and achievable choices about what you need to get done tomorrow.

Keep everyone in the loop. My colleagues at Four Seasons knew that I had a couple of rules about work on days I wasn't travelling. When in Toronto, I made it a rule to drive one of my kids to school in the morning. That meant I was generally unavailable for in-person meetings before 8:30 a.m. Plus, I always tried to be home before the kids fell asleep, to hear about their day and tell them I loved them. I'd often leave working dinners before dessert so that the kids could count on seeing me before bed. Of course, once they were teens the tables were reversed and it was they who dropped in on me to say goodnight!

Talk about the structure of work. In order for it to succeed, you have to be transparent with people about your approach to work–life integration. Part of that is ensuring that you have open discussions with your manager about how the structure of work at your company helps or hinders the advancement of women. If an organization says it's devoted to diversity and inclusion, what are they doing day in and day out that makes the difference? Each place has its own routines and flows — in fact it's sometimes the very bespoke nature of places and people that makes broad solutions difficult. But there's always going to be a thing or two — like those early morning meetings — that will cause a woman to say, "I can't do this anymore." In some circumstances, a conversation about it could be the difference between a woman staying with or leaving the workforce.

For decades we've been talking about advancing women and establishing policies in the workplace to ensure that it happens. We're hiring more women in the hope of creating a higher level of advancement for them. But the outcomes aren't changing as much as we expected them to as a result of all that effort. So, a conversation about what else needs to get done is now in order. We have a responsibility to ourselves — and to those who come after us — to do that.

Lorna Borenstein

FOUNDER AND CEO, GROKKER

Give Up the White Lie

Before I started my own business, I hadn't had any professional experiences in which I felt I could bring my whole self to work. There hadn't been enough of *me*; there was always a certain amount of "office armour" I had to put on in the morning.

So when I launched Grokker, a company focused on health and wellness, I wanted to create a "come as you are" environment for everyone at our headquarters in California. This is so important to me that when we're recruiting, I ask in the very first interview — before focusing on skills — "Where do you come from, what made you who you are, and what kind of environment do you thrive in?" I want to know these things so that we'll be able to cultivate the right team and create the right workplace.

I foster an environment that engages and embraces the whole person, including the personal. In fact, our top company value is "It's personal." As the founder and CEO, I must set the tone by living this value in plain sight for all to see. I'm a mother of three, and when I leave to attend a school event for, say, my daughter, I tell everyone where I'm going, how long I'll be out of touch, and when I'll be back.

We have to be ourselves, unafraid of judgment and yet accountable. Too often in the past I've heard people say, "I'm going to be taking off early today because I have an appointment." Why not just be honest and say "I'm going to be at my son's soccer game, I'll be gone 90 minutes, and then I'll be back online"? Why is it a crime to want to go to your kid's soccer game? We all need to have a life outside of work.

> "I FOSTER AN ENVIRONMENT THAT ENGAGES AND
> EMBRACES THE WHOLE PERSON. AS FOUNDER AND
> CEO, I MUST SET THE TONE BY LIVING THIS VALUE
> IN PLAIN SIGHT FOR ALL TO SEE.
>
> —*Lorna Borenstein*

So, give up the white lie. This will also help you manage what precious spare time you have. Are you the kind of person who often says yes when asked to do something you'd rather not? Do you make excuses to avoid disappointing others rather than just saying no? Consider giving the response you really want to rather than a white lie. Your feelings matter more than anyone else's.

Women especially need to hear this. I have a series of canned responses for the frequent requests I get from people asking for my time. For example, I might say, "Thank you so much for wanting me to be a part of your project/join your board, but I'm focusing my time and energy on my family, my current business, and my passion projects, so I will decline. Good luck with your search; it sounds like a very worthwhile idea."

It's empowering, and it's gutsy to be so honest. People have reacted incredibly positively because they feel I'm being truthful with them.

Margaret Heffernan

ENTREPRENEUR; CHIEF EXECUTIVE; AUTHOR

Margaret has written numerous books, including WILLFUL BLINDNESS (named by the FINANCIAL TIMES as one of the best business books of the decade) and her most recent book, BEYOND MEASURE: THE BIG IMPACT OF SMALL CHANGES. Her TED talks have been seen by more than eight million people. She advises private and public businesses and mentors senior and chief executives. Margaret spoke on the opening day of the 2018 Judy Project; what follows is an excerpt from that speech.

#MeToo: This Is Our Moment

The #MeToo movement has shaken me to my core; it's made me think not only about the real problem of harassment but also about the price we paid to enter the world of business.

We went into the workplace with an implicit deal. "Look, we'll be really nice. We'll behave. We'll wear stupid clothes to fit in and work stupid hours. Please just let us in." And they said, "Come on in and do the work. We're not going to pay you properly. And you may have to pay a price we're not going to talk about. But if you'll do that, well maybe you'll get an occasional opportunity." Even if we didn't know it, that's the deal we made.

I once ran a high-tech company in Boston backed by venture capitalists. I was the only female CEO in the 40 companies they backed. One day I discovered that I was being paid 50 percent less than all the other CEOs in the portfolio. I was sad and disappointed, and wasn't sure what to do about it. I sat down and wrote a long email to my boss. I spent a lot of time editing it, then editing it again, and kept editing it until it was just one sentence: "Dear David: I'm extremely disappointed to discover that I'm being paid 50 percent of what my male colleagues are being paid. Yours, Margaret." The next day, my pay was doubled.

It's interesting how reluctant I was to do that. I'd been a good girl all my career, and I'd had good rewards. I'd thought, *All this stuff they say about discrimination, it's not me.* And then, when it *was* me, I didn't feel entitled to be angry.

At my next company, I had to fire a guy because he was not very effective. Afterward several women told me, "We're so glad you fired John." Turns out he'd been a routine source of sexual harassment. When I asked these women why they hadn't told me before, they said, "We could see you had a lot on your plate."

To this day I look back and feel uncomfortable at the notion that this could have been going on and I didn't know about it. I've written a book called *Willful Blindness* — I'm supposed to understand this stuff. But I was wilfully blind in my own company.

Many years ago, I fell for the story that women weren't doing that well in corporate environments because there was a pipeline problem, a lack of ambition, the biological clock — all that stuff. And now we have to confront the idea that the one thing holding us back was that men didn't want us to be successful.

I think the great thing about #MeToo is that we're seeing a generation of women who feel they have every right in the world to work in a place that's safe and fair. #MeToo is a phenomenal opportunity that we mustn't let go of. It's big, it's public, it's unequivocal — and it's a moment we must not let go to waste.

I don't want to belong to a business world that says one thing and means another. I want to work for a company that says one thing and does it. That's not an exceptional demand; it's the same demand that society makes of companies if they're going to be trustworthy.

I'm tired of goodwill. I sit on a number of boards, and with every one I go in and say, "Okay, what are we doing differently now that we know this stuff is happening?" And someone says, "We have a policy." I say, "What are we doing about the policy? Are we discussing it? Do we have workshops to talk about how it works? And which board member is accountable for it? It can't be a woman, so which of you guys is going to stand up and say, 'I pledge that if anybody has a problem with this they can come to me with total confidentiality and I'll help them solve it'?"

> "#MeToo is a phenomenal opportunity.
> It's big, it's public, it's unequivocal —
> and it's a moment we must not let go
> to waste."
>
> —*Margaret Heffernan*

The big lesson of #MeToo is that you can't stamp out discrimination without allies. You have to have around you at work, and across your industry, friends and colleagues with whom you can be completely honest. Many people think they shouldn't have friends at work … that they should just come in, do the job, and leave. But we spend 100,000 hours in a career; you can't spend that much time friendless and still have a life, or be a truly functioning human being. So we need allies around us, especially allies who aren't like us. We need to make friends and allies of men and women, gay and straight, young and old, and from every culture and every denomination if we're going to show true leadership.

If the #MeToo movement shows us anything, it's that networks are more powerful than hierarchies. The power of women was achieved and articulated when they spoke to each other freely, openly, and without fear. You should regard this as a source of safety and power. You have the opportunity to use the network you've acquired at The Judy Project to be as honest — as ruthlessly honest — as you need to be about what's really happening to you and to people around you.

You'll never be able to do it alone. You'll always need each other — as sounding boards, as people to check your facts with, as people to get help and support from, as people to help you understand, "Where can I go and fix this? Where can I go and make it better? Who is it around me who needs the help that I can provide?"

Everybody is watching to see what we do: How much can we help each other? How much can we reach out and be honest and really put our shoulders to the wheel to make the world a better place? Because that's the only reason to have power.

3

Connection

onnection can mean many things. It can mean being connected to your own feelings, or being connected on an emotional level to other people, including people of different cultures. Being connected in this way to your employees, your colleagues, and your boss is important for leaders because you're not leading talent; you're leading human beings. When we know people at work as whole human beings and not just as a set of skills, there is a strong sense of appreciation. That makes us connected and engaged at work, driving a culture of openness and loyalty because we understand each other. And besides, when people bring their heart to work, the office is just a better place to be.

Connections also need to be formalized at times. No one gets to the top rungs of any organization without a little help from their friends. One big source of help comes from your network: your formalized connections. People sometimes dismiss networking as self-serving and artificial, but, as you'll read further on, you shouldn't underestimate its value. Effective networking is a key skill to develop if you're ambitious — and it's not a bad word! Check out the very concrete advice on building your network in this chapter.

Mentors are people who can support your skills development. They can be from your industry or your field of expertise, or they can just be a leader you admire. You can choose a mentor yourself

— you can ask anyone you believe you can learn from. Note to self: Go prepared. Ask questions, and if you have specific requests, get them ready. Remember that a mentor is generously paying their career opportunities forward by giving you guidance and advice. Use that advice judiciously.

Sponsors are different. They're people inside your organization who accept a long-term commitment to pull you up through the organization. Sponsors are not like mentors in another important way. You don't choose them; sponsors choose you (although you can ask them to choose you!), and their job is to help manage your career, build your skills, and represent you when you're not in the room. They'll speak up for you at the table when a job opportunity arises. If you want to perform at the highest level, you want a full arsenal — a robust network, great and varied mentors, and strong internal corporate sponsors.

Janet Kestin

CO-FOUNDER, SWIM

Open-Heart Policy

"You'd be really good at this job if you didn't wear your face on your face." I was new to the co–chief creative officer role at Ogilvy & Mather, and my boss felt the need to share this helpful observation after seeing me roll my eyes during a frustrating conversation with a client. I rolled my eyes, proving his point.

Everyone has an Achilles' heel. Mine has been my face. If I'm happy, you know it. Sad, thrilled, laughter too loud — and crying, god forbid — all the feelings flashing like neon signs. The behaviour that gets women labelled "emotional." And in business, emotional = unprofessional. But what if it doesn't? What if we've got it wrong and emotion is actually a secret weapon that creates deeper relationships among colleagues? With customers and clients? What if it's the key to connection and one of the meaningful underpinnings of success?

Years before the unfortunate eye-rolling incident, Barb, one of my most important clients, greeted me with "You look awful" as I arrived late to an early morning meeting. She and I were often at odds, and I wasn't sure how to respond. Let it slide? Make a little joke? Get on with the reason we were there? Or ...

"I spent the night in the hospital with my three-year-old son," I said as, to my horror, my eyes blurred with tears. "When I got to the babysitter's last night he was at the window waving. By the time I reached the front door, a fountain of blood was gushing from his head." He'd jumped off the couch straight into a glass coffee table. Fear. Hospital. Stitches. Mother guilt.

"Oh." She nodded with understanding. "I have a three-year-old boy and he's a holy terror, too." We spent a few minutes comparing the premature grey hairs that come from having boys who leap before they look, then carried on our business with a new sense of ease and the surprising first bricks of trust. It showed immediately in the work that followed.

I'd given her a peek into my life, she opened the door to her own. We suddenly saw each other as people, not functions, and it changed the dynamic between us forever after. Who knew that a simple human exchange had such power?

Me. I knew. I grew up in and out of the French-speaking community in Quebec, where open affection, grand gestures, dramatic feelings, and what we now call "oversharing" were the norm. When I came new to the workplace it was without armour, without one single clue about the codes of business culture, and I found that that openness was contagious — quick connective tissue. Except with the "titled." The closer to the corner office, the straighter the backs, the tighter the lips.

That's what it looked like to be at the top. So I started to mimic the behaviour of the grownups: the guys, and the rare woman who'd made it into their circle. *Those people* didn't fling their lives all over the boardroom table. Except for an occasional flash of anger, or the fist-pumping high that comes with a big win, they kept a lid on their emotions. Their tone was light or "business serious." To be like them, I needed to toughen up, shut down. I was told, "If you're a little girl, you have to be a big bitch to be taken seriously." So I closed my ears to my own inner voice, the one saying that showing emotion is valid, that feeling is okay.

Here's the problem with that: My relationships with coworkers and clients have been the difference between feeling joy and feeling misery. Success is a joint venture, and failure is less painful when you're not alone. I came to see that you can't truly connect when you put your feelings on ice.

The first time I spoke in public, it was at a client offsite. I and my art director partner, Nancy Vonk (whom you'll meet elsewhere in this book), had just won our first Cannes Lion — a fancy advertising industry award — for a campaign we'd done for Dove. I was invited to give a talk about what it took to come up with that idea and why the client–agency relationship was such an important piece of the puzzle. I wrote the speech, made the slides, and two days before the event came face to face with paralyzing stage fright. Even contemplating standing in front of a group of business people, dealing with a slide carrousel and a clicker, felt like stepping off a cliff. What if the technology failed? What if I couldn't remember my stuff? Lose the slides, I told myself. Fewer moving parts meant less could go wrong. But I still needed to show them something, right? So I sat on the floor of my office like a five-year-old, cutting images out of magazines to illustrate my points. I stuck them onto big sheets of construction paper, 17 in all, each with a headline. On the back of every sheet I wrote two or three words to remind myself of what I wanted to say.

When the day came, my legs were shaking so badly that instead of standing at the front of the room I pulled a small table close to the audience and sat on it cross-legged, the stack of rainbow-coloured paper in my lap. I flipped up those "slides" one at a time, dropped the formality of my prepared speech and just talked, inviting them into the conversation with me. When I finished, no one left the room. We just kept on talking. Human.

There's a management style called "leading by walking around," and it's exactly what it sounds like. My style was kind of like that. I tried not to default to email or even to the phone. As much as possible, I visited people, sat in their offices, listened, chatted, stayed caught up, let them into my life as they let me into theirs. Maybe that's why when a young employee was torn between following the woman he loved to another city and maybe giving up the career he loved or staying in Toronto and maybe giving up the woman, he came to my office to cry. People often came to my office to cry.

Genuine connection comes from an emotional place, a female place that's perceived to be a deficit, while men's grandfathered-in sternness, anger, toughness, and even rage are admired as "ruling with a firm hand." Boys will be boys and all that.

Well, I've come to believe that it's time for some *grandmothering* in. Here's what I imagine our grandmas, along with the most current management thinkers, would say:

Choose walking over texting. Listen better. Ask more questions. Talk less. Share more. Let an open-door policy become an open-heart policy. Try not to wear your face on your face quite so much. And remember that your heart has a place on your sleeve. It's how you connect. And connection is a superpower.

Daria Thorp

PRESIDENT, ADVANCED CHEMISTRY
DEVELOPMENT (ACD/LABS)

Overcoming Cultural Barriers

It's essential to understand how people from different cultures exhibit different behaviours. I can understand how crucial that is, having emigrated from Russia to Canada as a single parent when I was in my early thirties. I came with an excellent education, reasonable language skills, and a background in knowledge-based industries. However, I did not know the ways and habits of Canadians, or the cultural references — even the seemingly little things, like not having grown up watching the same cartoons and movies. More than that, I did not feel assured of success; being different and having an accent can do that.

We all bring our cultural habits with us, and managers everywhere must learn to deal with that diversity. As an immigrant myself, I've observed how a diversity of cultural backgrounds is reflected in a diversity of communication styles, attitudes to hierarchy, and work habits. Understanding that we all have cultural as well as individual differences is key. In fact, one of the biggest parts of my job is helping colleagues connect and integrate so that they can work well together.

Admittedly, it's not always easy. It calls to mind *The Magicians*, a classic Russian film in which a magician learns to walk through walls by adhering to this mantra: "Identify the goal, believe in yourself, discount the obstacle."

GOOD ADVICE
Extra Reading

Based on research that took place over a 40-year span in multiple countries, Geert Hofstede's *Cultures and Organizations: Software of the Mind* explores how national cultures differ and offers insights into making better cultural connections. As Jia Lin Xie, a professor at the University of Toronto's Rotman School of Management, puts it, "The book looks at the social norms by which people think, feel, and act, and examines how societal biases, such as stereotypes, affect diversity management."

One of the cultural dimensions Hofstede identifies as potentially shaping people's values, beliefs, and behaviour is "power distance": the extent to which the lower-ranking individuals of a society accept and expect power to be distributed unequally. "For example," Xie notes, "Canadian culture is characterized by low power distance while Chinese culture is higher in power distance."

Some management practices, she says, such as 360-degree feedback and participative leadership, originate in low-power-distance cultural backgrounds, and so would encounter challenges in a typical high-power-distance culture. Leaders, therefore, need to be sensitive to these differences, and prepare carefully before implementing such practices in a culturally diverse workforce.

Kimberly Armstrong

DEPUTY CITY MANAGER, EMPLOYEE SERVICES DEPARTMENT,
CITY OF EDMONTON

Making Emotional Connections

When it comes to connecting, never underestimate the value of an emotional attachment. It's so important to *like* people, and to be likable yourself. This often comes down to finding common interests, whether it's a love for Thai food or an interest in race cars.

Finding common ground can alter our career path. After all, when we're sitting around a boardroom table trying to figure out who'll get a promotion or who'll get to go on a course, the decision isn't always based on a candidate's competence alone. This is the real world — and much as we wish it were a meritocracy, it's not. Biases are real, and they impact our opportunities. Be honest: If you don't like someone, will you be their sponsor or stick up for them in a business meeting?

Many men have the advantage of making connections with other men through things like football conversations, golf outings, or an evening of wings and beer. Whatever the connection is, it gives them an advantage, resulting in things like a phone call about an opportunity that's come up.

These connections aren't always as easy for women to make, and they don't always come naturally. You have to be deliberate and intentional about making connections.

I worked with someone years ago whom I didn't like at all. No doubt the feeling was mutual. But we worked together all the time, so I knew I had to find something in common with him. Then I read somewhere that his daughter was an entrepreneur, and I've always been very interested in helping female entrepreneurs. So I let him know I'd heard about his daughter's work, and boom — we had a connection. I linked her with an entrepreneur group, and would ask my colleague about her often. My interest was genuine. That connection helped shift how I felt about working with him, and vice versa.

You can't always control who you're around at work, so you have to find emotional connections with people. I tell my team to make a list of five people they have a difficult relationship with and then make an effort to discover something in common. Walk into the person's office and look around. See what art they have up on the wall, what photos are on their desk … that's often all you'll need as a starting point.

Or try this: Before meetings, my team regularly does what I call a "round." We go around the room and people talk about how they're feeling today, what's on their mind — maybe their dog died, or their sister got engaged. Whatever it is people mention, you'll learn so much about your colleagues through these quick moments of sharing. "What are you watching on Netflix?" "What's on your iPod?" In other words, instead of assuming that connections will happen naturally, we can foster them.

Here's the thing: You can go to work unhappy every day, or you can do your best to find points of engagement with people. Be strategic and authentic about it. It's actually really easy to find common interests if you're intentionally open and present, and if you listen and learn.

GOOD ADVICE
Three Steps to Strategic Networking

When I attended The Judy Project in 2015, one strategy I got some great advice on was improving my networking skills. I've found over the years that it's a sure way to advance your career. I was in Ottawa on a course a few years ago when, out of the blue, I received a phone call inviting me to apply for a high-level position in my organization. That call would never have occurred if it weren't for someone in my network putting my name forward as a potential candidate; I'd never have considered doing that myself.

Networking isn't optional; it's essential. It does take time, but it's worth the investment. And I've found that the more you intentionally network, the more value your efforts will yield. Here's how to do it.

Diversify your network. Examine your network to identify where you can improve diversity. Does your network include the corporate sector, community organizations, and all levels of government? Is there representation from various age groups, genders, and cultural backgrounds?

I think of it this way: If I were fired tomorrow and reached out to my network the next day, would it have a broad enough reach? Because if everyone in my network knew everyone else, I'd be connecting with a much smaller group than if my network were distributed among different kinds of organizations and people.

So never hesitate to ask someone for their time, regardless of who it is and how experienced they may be. Remember: They haven't lived your life, they haven't seen what you've seen, they don't know what you know — and you have something to offer them as well.

Strengthen your network. Who do you want to add to your network? Maybe there's someone you already know who could give you an introduction to that person. Either way, here's how to reach out:

- Send them an "I'd love to take you for coffee" email. Offer to meet anywhere they choose to make it as easy as possible for them.

- Describe in the email why you want to meet; give them a hook, a reason to want to meet with you.

- Demonstrate that you've taken the time to research their background. You could mention something you have in common, such as having attended the same university or sharing a passion for a particular cause.

- Tell them specifically what you want to discuss, since the more clearly the person can picture why you're contacting them, the more likely they'll be to make the time.

And once you get the meeting, don't leave it without asking for another introduction! Weave into the discussion a request to be connected with someone else.

Network for your next role. Where do you want to be in five years, two years, even next year? What do you want to be doing? Develop a plan to connect with five people who might be able to help you achieve this.

Finally, in each discussion, give more than you take. It's a lesson I learned from Adam Grant's excellent book *Give and Take*. And listen. Being fully present for the conversation — mindful, aware, attentive — allows your insights, thoughts, and perspectives to flow. And in doing so you'll enrich, stretch, and maybe even ignite something within the other person.

—Kimberly Armstrong

Jane Kinney

VICE CHAIR, DELOITTE LLP

Four Steps to High-Value Networking

I've mentored and sponsored many, many women at Deloitte over the years. I make sure they're recognized, and that they get to the partnership level. It's a win-win, because attracting the best people to your team will result in greater success for yourself. Effective networking is definitely one of my strengths. It's part of my personal brand to be an integrator.

Networking can have negative connotations — as if it's all about trying to get something from someone. But at The Judy Project, I learned that networking is high value.

Here's how I do it.

1. **I use Outlook to keep track of people.** I'll put you in my contacts, and make a note of who you are and how we met. I keep people in my contacts even if I met them long ago. I don't forget people. If I made a good connection with a client 15 years ago I'll stay in touch, even if we no longer have a working relationship.

2. **I go out for lunch every day.** Whether it's with a colleague or someone I don't see regularly, daily lunch dates ensure that networking is part of my everyday routine. I never eat at my desk — that's boring. And besides, I enjoy making connections. At the moment I'm working with a major bank client, where there are hundreds of executives. I know most of them. Often I'll look at my list for someone I haven't talked to in a while and ask if they can join me for lunch.

3. **I try to find things we have in common.** We talk about work life and personal life. I share insights into what I'm seeing at work, and I ask them for their thoughts. I always try to find common ground. For example, because I like opera and ballet, I'll make a note of those with similar interests so that I can invite them sometime. I also ask my assistant to keep track of their kids' names and spouse's name.

4. **I started building my network when I was young.** I advise all young women to do this; it's so important. I'm still connected with women I worked with back in the 1980s. As you become more senior, so does your network. That means you'll have more connections.

Bill Thomas

GLOBAL CHAIR, KPMG

and

Mary Lou Maher

CANADIAN MANAGING PARTNER, QUALITY AND RISK MANAGEMENT, KPMG

Putting Women in Line
for Leadership

Bill: Very early in my term we made a conscious decision to focus on gender diversity. We'd been great at it below the partner level, but we had a long way to go at the partner level. The management team and the board all had to honestly acknowledge that the road for a woman and the road for a man weren't the same, certainly not in our business.

Mary Lou: In terms of the proportion of women and men we hire at our firm, it's 50-50 here in Canada and stays that way up to the senior manager level. Then the number of women drops: the ratio above that up to partner is 32 to 68. And at partner level, it's 27 percent women.

Bill: To make a difference, we had to be clear on our own motivations, and mine was easy: I have two daughters and a son, and when they were small, under age 10, I remember thinking it made no sense that my son would have a better opportunity to succeed at KPMG (or any other company) than his two sisters would.

As the CEO, I felt that not only did I have an opportunity, but that it was my responsibility to do something about that. I had to have the strength and the guts as a leader to stand up in front of my team and honestly articulate our path to a different outcome. And I had to convey that this wasn't a conversation about, by, and for women — it was a conversation that should be about, by, and for everyone.

Mary Lou: That was three years ago, when we introduced the Women in Line for Leadership program. It was based in part on learnings from The Judy Project, and focused on every manager who wanted to be a partner. We give more support to women earlier in their careers, such as with on-ramps and off-ramps for mat leaves. We want to ensure that partners represent the wider community from a diversity perspective. Since we put the spotlight on the problem, we've seen a clear improvement: women now represent 40 percent of those in the pipeline to make partner.

Encouraging sponsorships is making the biggest difference. When Bill became CEO, he launched a new sponsorship program that assigned the firm's top 30 female partners to sponsors on the executive committee.

What's more, when senior managers are in line for promotion to partner, they're assigned a sponsor to ensure that they're successful in obtaining that promotion.

But I said we can't have women be the only ones responsible for it. The company has to deal with things like unconscious bias training. This opened a lot of eyes. Many people think it's the colleagues across the table who are the ones with bias, "not me." But they realize through the training that they have those biases, too.

Bill: We've had to recognize the inherent bias in individuals and in the firm as a whole. That's been about having very honest conversations around this fact: that the path is different for men than it is for women.

Marlene Cepparo

PARTNER, KPMG

Helping Others Move Up

One of the most generous and important things you can do as a leader is to care enough, and to put in the time, to develop the next generation. The part of my job that delights me immensely is seeing one of my senior managers become a partner, or hearing someone tell me that I made a difference to their career. Being a good mentor is easy once you realize that everyone is really good at something, and all you have to do is figure out what that something is — and then step out of the way as they shine.

Of course, finding that special quality takes time and patience. For example, in my line of work, teaching someone the importance of the detail required in developing a tax plan isn't always easy, but once they've done it, you've got someone who can do it the next time. And it's not just about their learning the technical aspects of something; it's also about giving them the credit and the exposure to help develop them into gurus. It's giving them the support to fulfill their potential.

This is what my mentor did for me. We worked on a complex reorganization, and then he had me present it. He attributed more value to what I did than I felt I deserved. But it gave me the profile to get others asking me questions, and helped me develop so that I could eventually do it myself.

Currently, I'm working with someone who I see making partner in a few years. She's a bit of a quiet personality, and she needs to build her profile and let people know she can do it. So, together we developed a plan in which, at key group meetings, she discusses a tax issue and the potential answer, and seeks feedback from the group. Our plan is for her to do this at every meeting so that people get to know who she is as she demonstrates her technical expertise. The intention is to help her find her own voice, to demonstrate her capabilities in a way that she feels comfortable. Getting her to the next generation is one of my next goals.

Not long ago I was working with a junior person who was really smart, but he just didn't pay enough attention to the details — and you can't prepare a good tax return if you gloss over details! So I reviewed his returns and gave him the frank feedback he needed. And guess what? He understood what needed to be done, even if maybe he didn't like it, and became very good at it. When he later left to take on a consulting role, he gave me a card thanking me for the time I'd spent helping him become more detail oriented. That was important to me because, even though I'd made the effort to improve him, I thought he felt I'd been a little tough on him. In reality, he, too, saw it as a good thing. He is now a CFO.

So while giving your time to help someone improve isn't always easy, when approached with genuine care and openness, it's well worth it. Helping others in that way, as I've been helped, makes me smile.

GOOD ADVICE
Get Yourself a Sponsor

One of the ways I've actively managed my career — and a key factor in becoming a leader — is by having sponsors at eBay's head office in California. My sponsors have been people several levels above me who were willing to advocate on my behalf, which is critical when you work in a remote market.

How do you get sponsors? I've found that you have to take the initiative and have very direct, transactional conversations with potential sponsors: "Are you willing to champion me?" The first time I had one of these conversations, it was nerve-racking. But, inevitably, I've found support and encouragement — these leaders have had the same conversations with their own sponsors.

For your sponsors to be effective, you need to provide them with information they can use to tell your story; you need to arm them with facts and figures so that they can advocate for you when decisions get made about who will get the next big role. This type of active sponsorship has been tremendously impactful in terms of my advancement at eBay.

—Andrea Stairs
General Manager, eBay Canada & Latin America

Denise Pickett

CHIEF RISK OFFICER AND PRESIDENT,
GLOBAL RISK, BANKING AND COMPLIANCE,
AMERICAN EXPRESS

The Power of Connection

I've learned that being sponsored, and acting as a sponsor to pull people up the hill, is one of most important things you can do. I've certainly championed others over the years, and, as for me, I wouldn't be sitting where I am today if not for Ed Gilligan, the late vice chairman and president of American Express. When I put my hand up for the job of country manager for Canada in 2007, Ed was one of the key decision makers who took a chance on me. Later, a position in one of the biggest divisions in the U.S. came up — and there was Ed, asking me, "How do you feel about moving?" Ed helped me see that I can do things I'd never done before. That's the power of connection. Not only do you need to believe in yourself, you need sponsorship.

And those sponsors can also help you stay true to yourself. Another sponsor gave me some excellent advice when I was about to move to HQ. I was questioning whether my personality — specifically my sense of humour — would fit in with the corporate office culture after running headquarters from Toronto. I'm an extrovert; I like to engage with people in any environment at any time. But my sponsor quickly explained that my authenticity as a leader was ultimately what helped me get the job in the first place.

Rowena Chan

HEAD OF DISTRIBUTION, INDIVIDUAL INSURANCE AND WEALTH
& PRESIDENT, SUN LIFE FINANCIAL DISTRIBUTORS INC.

How My Sponsor Pushed Me into the Spotlight

A couple of years ago, I was working behind the scenes on a national diversity initiative for TD, leading a team in preparing for the key launch event. An executive leader asked me to be the emcee, since I'd led this initiative from the start.

I hesitated at the opportunity. Although I'd been the architect of this and other similar initiatives, I preferred to feature other talent and avoid the spotlight.

My hesitation was rooted in two persistent professional barriers I encountered as a first-generation Canadian. The first barrier was language.

> "WE ALL BRING OUR CULTURAL HABITS WITH US, AND MANAGERS EVERYWHERE MUST LEARN TO DEAL WITH THAT DIVERSITY."
> —*Daria Thorp*

I was born and raised in Hong Kong, and although I was fluent in English, my first language was Cantonese, so I had to focus on making sure my communications were clear, concise, and professional. To help myself constantly improve my communication skills, I kept — and still keep — a folder in Outlook called "Communications," where I shamelessly save well-delivered messages from others that inspire me. I also find *Say It Like Obama*, a book on President Barack Obama's oratory skills, incredibly helpful.

But language wasn't my only challenge in the workplace; cultural differences also played a major role. I was raised in a Chinese culture that maintains a belief that good work simply speaks for itself. My upbringing emphasized not being the centre of attention, but rather suppressing oneself and being one of the crowd.

> **"YOU CAN'T ALWAYS CONTROL WHO YOU'RE AROUND AT WORK, SO YOU HAVE TO FIND EMOTIONAL CONNECTIONS WITH PEOPLE."**
>
> —*Kimberly Armstrong*

This belief became especially important to overcome as I assumed leadership roles, because you need to articulate your vision in compelling and passionate ways so that you inspire your people and bring them along the journey.

After I declined the emcee role, my executive sponsor persisted. She could see I needed a boost in taking that step. "I still want you to consider it. You don't have to do it, but you're always celebrating others before yourself. You deserve to demonstrate that you led this." It was an attitude shared by another great manager of mine, who told me that her job was to "push me into the fishbowl so that others can see what I see in you."

I thought hard about my sponsor's emcee proposal, and ultimately concluded that I should do it. I needed to continue to push myself outside my comfort zone and to be courageous in advocating for myself and my work.

4

Compassion

We spend over half of our lives at work, with our corporate families. Yet some people still think that the values you uphold as a human being should be somehow different at work than they are at home. Why should that be? Why should you be kind and generous at home but an inconsiderate asshole at work? It doesn't make sense in today's world. It's good to be compassionate at home *and* at work. Men and women who are fortunate to have had a good home life already know that.

Yet in today's society, it's easier for women to express this characteristic in our leadership style than it is for men. This can be an underestimated opportunity. In the workplace, compassion is the demonstration of care combined with a vow to do something about it. If you can demonstrate it well and in an authentic way, people will want to reciprocate. Each story in this chapter shows how compassionate leadership creates a culture in which people are engaged and motivated.

Paula Knight

VICE PRESIDENT, PEOPLE, STRATEGY AND
COMMUNICATIONS, CANCER CARE ONTARIO

The Surprise in
My Envelope

Soon after I completed The Judy Project program, my three-year-old son was diagnosed with cerebral palsy and autism. That put the future into question. Throughout my career, I'd always planned where I wanted to be in five years. I thought maybe I had a future in advancing to the U.S. with Microsoft. But now, with this devastating news, I wondered if should give up my career altogether. Then I remembered that every one of the high-powered women I'd talked to at The Judy Project had experienced a life event and faced similar decisions. So I knew that while life would be different from what I'd planned, I could shape it in a way that would create a balance between caring for my children and continuing to feed my sense of purpose through my work. Perhaps the two things could align.

That's when two people sent me a posting for a job at Cancer Care Ontario. I questioned whether I was a fit for the role. After all, I didn't have a background in health care. But one of the women I met at The Judy Project disagreed. "This job is a gift for you," she said. She was talking about a quality I had never fully appreciated in myself until I went through one of The Judy Project's classic exercises. We had to ask colleagues and friends to write something about us. I tend to be very harsh on myself, so I was very surprised to read what a colleague at Microsoft had written:

Paula has an innate ability to connect with people and cares deeply about making a difference in their lives. One of her greatest strengths is never losing sight of the fact that at the centre of all the technology work she does is another human being. Paula only ever talks about what the technology will now help people do, be it a child who is blind reading a book in digital format for the first time or law enforcement officers being able to work together to combat child exploitation and rescue more children. She reminds us all of our collective purpose.

The letter was a gift. It helped me see myself with more clarity, and it helped me deal with the crisis that came soon after. I realized that the role at Cancer Care Ontario did speak to my skill set. I had the courage to go for it, and I am very grateful I did.

Aileen Kheraj

VICE PRESIDENT, CREDIT CARD PRODUCTS, LOYALTY, AND ACCOUNT MANAGEMENT, AT TD

Through Thick and Thin

My husband and I moved to New York from Toronto in 2005 when he got a new opportunity with his firm in the banking sector. As such, I was working under an L2 visa, which essentially meant that I could legally work in the United States as long as my husband continued to be employed with his bank. I joined American Express under these parameters.

Fast-forward to March of 2009. Now we had a 20-month-old son and were in the thick of the financial crisis. My husband, along with so many others, had been displaced from his bank — which meant I could no longer legally work in the U.S.

I had begun reporting to a new leader less than a couple of months prior. Now I'd have to tell her I'd be leaving Amex and moving back to Canada in the next week. I'd have to figure out my next career move then. The prospect of both my husband and I having no income, not to mention the fact that we had a child and didn't know where we'd be living back in Toronto, was of course incredibly stressful.

I walked into my leader's office to give her the news — and her response completely surprised me. She asked for 24 hours to figure something out. She, too, had a new leader running the division, and wanted to explore options with her.

The next day my boss told me, "Go to Canada. Take your company computer and call me when you're settled. I don't know yet if you're going to be a Canadian or a U.S. employee of Amex, but you'll continue to be an employee. We'll figure it out. Don't worry about a thing." I couldn't believe it.

So we packed up our stuff into a truck and moved home. Thankfully, one of my girlfriends from MBA school, who was on maternity leave at the time, had volunteered to check out places with a realtor, and had helped us secure a place to live — sight unseen.

We got back to Toronto on a weekend and I started working from home on the Monday. I was still working for the U.S., but had been transferred to the Canadian business unit. Then, in 2010, an opportunity came up to work in the Canadian organization. Eight years later, I've progressed in my career within the Canadian division of Amex, leading the Consumer Lending & Member Engagement team.

The compassion of my direct leader, and of those she tapped into for support for me, is something that to this day I'll never forget, and am forever grateful for — so much so that when I got the chance to pay it forward to one of my direct reports, I didn't hesitate.

That team member was a pivotal contributor, consistently delivering strong results regardless of the challenges she was given. One day she told me that her mother, with whom she was very close, had been diagnosed with terminal cancer. She asked for the flexibility to assume the role of primary caregiver, and said she may need to take a leave to tend to her mother's care.

I told her to take whatever time she needed, to work from home whenever she wanted, and to not hesitate to step out for appointments for her mom. I also offered to take some of the work off her plate, but she never took me up on that part.

"**The unexpected benefit of compassionate leadership is that it creates an immeasurable degree of loyalty and an even deeper engagement among team members to deliver their very best.**"

—*Aileen Kheraj*

About six months went by, and her mother passed away. This team member is now one of my most dependable directors. She has expressed deep and sincere gratitude for the unconditional flexibility and support. To be honest, I thought I was simply doing what was right; after all, my leader had demonstrated caring and compassion for me when I needed it most.

The unexpected benefit of compassionate leadership is that it creates an immeasurable degree of loyalty and an even deeper engagement among team members to deliver their very best.

Maria Theofilaktidis

EXECUTIVE VICE PRESIDENT, CHIEF COMPLIANCE AND
REGULATORY OFFICER, SCOTIABANK

My Father's Daughter

As a senior leader in my organization, I often get asked what drives me. I think it's a story my father first shared with me when I was in elementary school, and to this day I can't tell it without getting emotional.

My parents were from very poor farming families on the Mediterranean island of Cyprus. Neither had any formal education, and both had started working at a young age to support their families. They emigrated to Johannesburg, South Africa, for a better life.

When I was born, my father went to a government office in Johannesburg to register my birth. His English wasn't very good, so he couldn't fill in the form. But when he asked for help the people working in the office started laughing at him, shaming him. In fact, one sarcastically told him that he should have gone to school before having a baby! He was embarrassed and upset, and responded protectively: "I came to this country for a better life. I hope one day this little baby girl grows up to be more successful than all of you!" (or at least something akin to this). A lady in the office took pity on him and filled in the form.

I will always remember my roots in the context of how my father was made to feel that day. I never want to make anyone feel the same thing. I focus on respecting all individuals for the value they bring to the team, regardless of role or education or status.

This humility and compassion are key, and I'm not very tolerant of people who don't work that way.

Most importantly, I want people to feel valued for who they are and what they are.

And there's also this: I want to prove my dad was right about his hopes for me that day in the birth registry office, over and over again. I want to vindicate him, and make all his sacrifices worthwhile.

Sandra Rondzik Popik

VICE PRESIDENT AND CEO, CIBC LIFE INSURANCE

Making It Personal

Drive. Focus. Goals. Results. These are just some of many business imperatives, just some of the many critical elements of future success. But how about kindness? Caring? Being personal?

I used to be, and continue to be, very results focused. While I see this as important, I've learned that work is not just about *what* we do, it's also about *how* we do it. And two particularly defining moments of my career helped me realize how critical the human element is in everything we do.

The first came fairly early on, when a colleague pulled me aside to share some feedback. I didn't think he'd had enough of a chance to see me in action, so I was a little skeptical. However, I'd always held him in high regard and was appreciative that he wanted to connect. All I remember from our entire conversation was him saying, "People are sometimes intimidated by you. You don't have to be all business all the time." My initial — inner — reaction was,

You bet I'm all business all the time! That's how I get results. That's how I get things done. That's a good thing … isn't it?

I went home that day and actually had to think about whether he was praising my results-focused style or giving me constructive feedback on how to do things better. I didn't get it. *All business all the time* was so ingrained in my mind and my approach that I didn't even think about how that may have been coming across. But after some reflection, I understood: The minute people arrived at one of my meetings, I'd go straight to the business at hand … no time "wasted" with "How was your weekend?" or "How is your family?" In retrospect, I could certainly have taken a moment to ask such questions. Don't get me wrong. I had always sincerely cared about the people I worked with; it's just that I was too focused on "efficiently" getting to business. It took this feedback to realize that I wasn't always projecting my true desire for connection and maintained too big of a separation between "business" and "personal." We need people to support us, to work with us to achieve common goals. That can be done effectively only if we genuinely care about them, and if we *show* we care through our words and our actions. I'm glad I got this lesson so early in my career.

> **"WE NEED PEOPLE TO SUPPORT US, TO WORK WITH US TO ACHIEVE COMMON GOALS. THAT CAN BE DONE EFFECTIVELY ONLY IF WE GENUINELY CARE ABOUT THEM, AND IF WE SHOW WE CARE THROUGH OUR WORDS AND OUR ACTIONS."**
>
> —*Sandra Rondzik Popik*

The other moment came when my VP said something that made me stop and really think. I was explaining a rather complex business challenge — something that involved consulting multiple business partners, synthesizing key facts, pulling out the most critical figures, and outlining options, implications, and recommendations. I mentioned that I'd responded to one of our more contrarian business partners with "It's nothing personal, it's just business." My manager stopped me mid-sentence and said, slowly and clearly: "Sandra, it's *all* personal." I paused. I reflected. This was *not* where I'd been expecting our conversation to go. Perhaps I even expected to be praised for the great job I'd done managing the complex issue. My whole approach was being challenged. But, of course, I realized he was right. How could I not have seen it? I was dealing with people. Everything we do is about people; how could it not be personal? It was this short, quick comment that completely altered how I look at work. It's essential that we remember the human element behind everything we do — and not be afraid to make it personal.

THE MOMENT

My manager stopped me mid-sentence and said, slowly and clearly: "Sandra, it's *all* personal." It was this short, quick comment that completely altered how I look at work. It's essential that we remember the human element behind everything we do — and not be afraid to make it personal.

While drive, focus, goals, and results are all critical components of our business lives, so is the underlying, noncompromising element of being human. We can't lose our humanity in the world of business. As our CEO, Victor Dodig, once said, "Don't leave your hearts at home when you come to work." The only way we can inspire the hearts and minds of our teams is by taking the time to be kind and caring. So, go ahead: Make it personal.

Lorna Borenstein

FOUNDER AND CEO, GROKKER

The Compassionate Workplace

I think you have to lead by example, and one of the things I want my company to be is compassionate. About four years ago, my mom was diagnosed with cancer. I told everyone at Grokker that I'd be less present for a few months as I spent time taking her for consultations, surgery, and then moving her post-surgery from Montreal to live with me in California so that I could help her during her chemo treatments. While undergoing chemo she even came to work occasionally (wearing her turban!).

If I were working anywhere else, I would have had to tell my boss, "I need to take some personal days for medical reasons, but don't worry, I won't let anything slip." It would have been all about assuaging their fears about my not performing as well rather than about supporting me through a difficult few months. That's not putting people first. That's not compassion. The openness with which I shared my mother's situation was met by remarkable kindness and warmth. My team learned firsthand that they just have to share what's happening in their lives and they will be supported.

A few months ago, one of our engineers in the Midwest told his manager he just wasn't feeling himself, that he was sad and despondent. He said he'd never felt that way before, and didn't know what was happening. It took a lot of guts and honesty on his part to tell his manager. His manager showed compassion, and said, "Would you feel comfortable talking to Lorna about this? Because I think we can help you."

He agreed. It was clear to me that he was depressed, so I encouraged him to see a therapist. We also arranged to have weekly calls as a bit of extra support. I wanted him to know that he wasn't alone, that he was brave, and that we at Grokker fully supported what he was doing for himself.

> **"MY TEAM LEARNED FIRSTHAND THAT THEY JUST HAVE TO SHARE WHAT'S HAPPENING IN THEIR LIVES AND THEY WILL BE SUPPORTED."**
> —*Lorna Borenstein*

The therapist helped, as did things like physical movement, scheduling short walks, and journalling to practise gratitude about the good things in his life. But the improvements weren't enough, so we encouraged him to see a psychiatrist and consider medication. This idea was foreign to him; he never would have taken that initiative on his own. But he dared to try it — and, three weeks later, on one of our weekly calls, he said he was starting to feel better. Then, a month later, he said he was actually beginning to feel like himself again, and felt that he had things to look forward to.

I will never forget the day, not long after that, when he told me he was "totally okay." He still is. And he posted his experience on Facebook to let everyone know that mental illness isn't embarrassing or something to be ashamed of — that it happened to him and he got help. He said he'd realized that taking prescription meds to help with mental health is akin to getting a prescription for eyeglasses to help your vision.

To have a compassionate workplace — where you don't have to worry about your job being at stake if difficulties come up, where you know your colleagues will help you — should be the norm.

5

Energy

*P*art of the leader's job is to deliver positive energy to the team so they'll believe that what you're asking them to do is possible. If you can set the stage this way, people can deliver remarkable performance. But it has to start with you, the leader. You have to get rid of negative energy, such as anger, and discover the source of positive energy inside yourself. This might sound as though it comes from a weekend with a self-help guru, but it isn't. Just think of how two very different bosses might approach an employee. The first one says, "You're always screwing up." The second one says, "You can do it!" Who would get a better result?

Q&A

Ikram Al Mouaswas

Partner, Deloitte LLP

Q. **In a corporate setting, why does it help to be happy?**

A. People talk about how you have to believe in yourself, and that's true. But I think it's all about making sure you do whatever it takes to be happy in your life. If you're a happy person, you'll be motivated to perform well. You'll want to help others, and you'll create positive energy all the time, so people will *want* to work with you. That means you'll get more experience, and therefore you'll get promotions. The happiness cycle is incredible, and self-perpetuating: be happy, and all the other good things that come will be beautifully linked to that.

Q. **So how do *you* be happy?**

A. I made a conscious decision long ago to always create the best version of myself. Acting in your own best interest isn't selfish; it adds value to the community around you, whether among your friends, home, or work community. And if you make it mandatory to be your best, you can achieve that. For example, if you feel that to be your best you have to have an organized bedroom, then you must organize your bedroom. When it comes to daily exercise, don't think of it as a choice; you simply have to do it. Same thing goes with nutrition: you must make healthy meals rather than resorting to fast food. Every single thing in your life has to be the best for you. When you tell yourself you don't have a choice in the matter, there are no temptations, and it's easier.

Plus, I set personal goals that are measurable, whether it's fitness — such as holding a plank position for a certain amount of time — or reaching a particular goal at work. Orient yourself toward something measurable.

Q. **How does this attitude play out in your role as a leader?**

A. I'm very proud that my teams seem to be the happiest around. People from other departments say, "You're the one with the happy team." They ask me how we make that happen, and I tell them that it's in the small, everyday, simple changes we can make. For example, we don't allow any junk food in the office; when we're working overtime I offer an unlimited food budget — but only if it's healthy foods. And even when we're in our extremely busy period, we don't work past 11 p.m. We mandate that everyone on the team always gets at least six hours of sleep each night. In terms of exercise, we've created a board that team members can add tick marks to whenever they've done a workout. We do Pilates together some mornings before work.

I pitch to them all that these physical changes lead to mental wellness, and that you can get addicted to the endorphins. Some people resist at first, but then it's remarkable how everyone's mood improves when they try these things. We exude positive energy daily, and it's contagious. It can lead to team members getting a shot at being the next big leader.

Q. **How does that work?**

A. I'll never forget a young woman on my team who exemplifies that. A couple of years ago, on a sunny September morning, the two of us had a breakfast meeting at America Restaurant, on the thirty-first floor of what was then called the Trump Tower. It was a regular one to one. Over eggs benny — mine — and yogurt with granola — hers — she told me she wanted a promotion in a year. That would be one year earlier than she'd normally be considered to move to the next level.

I'd recently offered her a spot to lead a new team with me. On her previous team she'd been used to working too late and feeling very stressed. She was sweet and a great worker, but had been quiet and normally kept to herself. I was starting to see that she was learning about the way I like to lead. Her confidence was grow- ing, and her dedication to health and fitness was as well. So I was pleasantly surprised to learn she had that kind of ambition.

I told her it would be exceptional to be promoted so early, but that I was more than happy to set this goal and work on it together. So we'd talk weekly about what I wanted her to think about, and how to think about it. Part of that was creating a happy team around her so that all the missions we needed to achieve would naturally cascade. We talked about how to organize and project-manage.

The impact I saw on her team was beautiful. Team members started to look up to her; some told me, "My goal is to be like her." That is a definition of a great leader — because, of course, leaders are followed. And within a few months her reputation grew, with other partners letting me know how great she was doing. Needless to say, she earned the promotion.

Q. **Any final thoughts on how leadership can impact employees' lives?**

A. You have to remove barriers that might be holding people back from being their best and trying new things. For example, Deloitte is a major sponsor of Ride to Conquer Cancer, a two-day, 200-kilometre bike ride that supports cancer research. I recently joined the leadership team on that, and we had to figure out ways to get more people to participate. So when staff would say things like "But it's too long, where will I stay overnight?" we got discounted hotel rooms for everyone and organized a mid-weekend dinner to celebrate. And when we heard things like "But I'll never be able to raise the minimum $2500 donation," we went to the partners — and they all donated money to help staff make up funds where they were short. We went from 150 participants from our office to 250 the next year. And we're set to grow again.

Removing barriers, and creating an experience in your workplace that encourages participation, are key. When people can integrate overall happiness into everything they do, it always leads to more energy and, ultimately, more success.

Dawn Jetten

PARTNER, BLAKE, CASSELS & GRAYDON LLP

The Power of Positive Energy

Early in my career, with a young family and a very demanding legal practice, I found myself caught up in discussions with female colleagues and girlfriends about our various problems: too much work, not enough help, childcare issues, outstanding house repairs, not enough time for anything. These conversations came up anywhere and everywhere. They happened at work, during lunch, on late-night calls with family and friends. They happened at hockey arenas. They even happened poolside — no, not anywhere exotic, but at my kids' swimming lessons.

In the midst of one, well, bitch session, one of my friends laughed and said, "We really shouldn't talk to each other."

That has always stayed with me. It's when I realized that while these kinds of conversations are helpful — beyond venting, they're a way to learn that others are dealing with the same challenges — they can make you start to feel as though everyone is overwhelmed and that there are no good solutions.

So instead of participating in what sometimes felt like competitive complaining, I learned to focus on how people were dealing with these issues. From then on, I made a conscious effort to ask for advice rather than complain.

I intentionally focused on the question of why I stayed in my job when I could find a different, less demanding one, either in the field of law or outside of it. In my mind, I articulated the things I loved about my job: The interesting and challenging work. Opportunities to learn new things. And working with intelligent, motivated people.

> "IN THE MIDST OF ONE OF OUR, WELL,
> BITCH SESSIONS, ONE OF MY FRIENDS
> LAUGHED AND SAID, "WE REALLY SHOULDN'T
> TALK TO EACH OTHER." FROM THEN ON,
> I MADE A CONSCIOUS EFFORT TO ASK FOR
> ADVICE RATHER THAN COMPLAIN."
>
> —*Dawn Jetten*

These internal conversations reminded me of why continuing to pursue a successful career at Blakes was the right thing for me. They also helped me identify (1) the things I could build on, (2) the things I could change, and (3) the things I would just have to live with. Since then, whenever I've felt overwhelmed by competing demands, returning to this focus has been very helpful.

I've had the same internal conversation about lots of things that add stress: Why put the kids in another activity, why sign up for this committee or that volunteer position, why commit to this event with friends? Simply knowing the answers helps me determine priorities, deal with the challenges, and enjoy what I do.

Jennifer Gillivan

PRESIDENT AND CEO, IWK FOUNDATION

The Secret Power of Forgiveness

Remember when Michelle Obama said "When they go low, you go high"? That's the sentiment of the story I want to share with younger women concerning something we don't hear a lot about: forgiveness.

Years ago, forgiving someone who'd done me wrong proved to be a defining moment in my career. I was badly treated by another female leader, and it hurt — both professionally and personally. She sent an apology in writing, but I didn't feel closure. I couldn't sleep, and was unsure how to continue with her. She had actually behaved inappropriately toward me for several years; it was a hurtful pattern that I didn't know how to come back from.

I confided in a respected CEO who was a mentor to me, and I'll never forget her advice: "You have two choices. You have every reason to complain to HR and make the other person feel terrible, because what she did was shameful. But you also have a much harder choice, and that is to forgive her, face to face. That doesn't mean you don't hold her accountable, but it does mean you're not going to carry this incident with you."

People never talk about forgiveness in business and leadership, but it's through forgiveness that you take back power. I thought it over for a few days, and made my decision. I walked into her office, acknowledged her written apology, and then told her straight out, and genuinely, that I forgave her for her behaviour. She was embarrassed. She hadn't been expecting this, and it was a profound moment for us both. The result was that we came to respect each other and work successfully together.

In that moment, I'd never felt more empowered. This was a very big lesson: that bad things happen, but by holding people accountable for their actions *and* forgiving them, you let go of the negative energy — and release any power they have over you.

THE MOMENT

In that moment, I'd never felt more empowered. By holding people accountable for their actions *and* forgiving them, you let go of the negative energy — and release any power they have over you.

GOOD ADVICE
10 Lessons for Success

Judy Elder created energy for a roomful of captivated women the day she gave her "Ambition" speech, and it has very obviously had a ripple effect. That energy is a key element of The Judy Project program each year — I know, because I've been fortunate enough to attend. And ever since, through speeches, presentations, and one-on-one conversations, I've harnessed Judy's energy and shared with others her lessons about success — and they have everything to do with owning all that you do.

1. **Own your ambition.** Go for the promotion, take risks in your career, and make different choices that suit you.

2. **Own the room.** Sit in the middle of the boardroom table and take a position of leadership and power.

3. **Own your authenticity.** Be yourself. Find your tribe, but don't conform. Don't try to be a version of what others want from you; remain true to yourself.

4. **Own your values.** Be who you really are; be true to where you've come from.

5. **Own your voice.** First, find your voice. Then learn how to do effective public speaking and presentations. If you're invited into a senior room, make sure you say something and be a part of the conversation.

6. **Own your decisions.** If something works, great — take the credit. If it doesn't work, then take the fall and learn from the mistakes you've made. Never let others take the fall for you.

7. **Own your courage.** Do the right thing, always. Fight against injustice; expect to be treated equally and paid equally for the work you do. If you don't get that respect, claim it, fight for it, talk about it — make the change.

8. **Own those coming behind you.** Remember to pay it forward. It's the only way we can improve life for us all, especially for women.

9. **Own those who went before you.** Always be grateful; thank people who helped you. And don't forget them as you climb the ladder of life and career.

10. **Own where you are.** Don't talk about what you don't have; be grateful for what you do have. Bloom right where you're planted, and it's amazing what will grow.

—Jennifer Gillivan

Emma Da Silva

VICE PRESIDENT, MICROSOFT CANADA

When Energy Lifts You Up

There I was in Sault Ste. Marie, Ontario, camping with friends and taking a well-earned break, blissfully unaware that my career was about to take a path I'd never in a million years guessed it would. I was happily working for Microsoft as an accountant. I envisioned a trajectory where, just as I'd met my education goal of becoming a CPA, I'd climb in the area of finance and one day meet my biggest goal: becoming a CFO.

So far, everything was going exactly to plan — my plan. But one of the VPs, Frank Clegg, had different ideas, and I was about to be energized in a new way. Frank and I had recently worked on a project together. My work must have had an impact on him, because while I was happily sipping a cold drink lakeside, he'd put my name into the hiring process for a business manager job. I'd soon be learning about business operations, marketing, and so much more.

I'd heard about the business manager position before I went on holiday, but didn't consider applying for it; I knew people who were more qualified, and I lacked the confidence to think I could compete with them. Don't get me wrong: I'd never had any lack of confidence in school. I'd been an athlete, and knew I could win if I trained hard. But I just didn't feel I was ready for this position that I was now being surfaced for. It proves that if men think they're 75 percent prepared for something they go for it, while women feel we have to be 110 percent prepared.

I got the position. And whenever I thought I was in over my head, my boss would tell me every day that he had confidence in me. His energy was infectious. I thrived in the role, and began to recognize in myself what others were seeing in me.

There's something about confidence that creates more energy. It finally dawned on me: I'd been holding back. I could actually do the things I hadn't thought I could. It moved me forward on the risk-aversion plane: I could see my potential and use the opportunity to challenge myself. It changed how I saw my career, and even my personal life. I became fascinated by taking on new challenges. In fact, I went back to playing competitive water polo; I'd made the national team at age 18, but had given it up after finishing university so that I could focus on my career. But now I had the drive to do new things and not pour all my energy into just one bucket.

I'd also assumed that my career would be based in Canada. But now I no longer saw geography as an obstacle. I became open to exploring, and ended up spending most of my time in the U.S. over four years, moving across the businesses we were covering down there. That really opened up my world.

> "WHEREAS BEFORE I'D WALK INTO A ROOM AND APPROACH ONLY THE PEOPLE I KNEW, NOW I DO THE OPPOSITE. I LOOK FOR NEW PEOPLE TO CONNECT WITH."
>
> —*Emma Da Silva*

Socially, too, I became more assertive. Whereas before I'd walk into a room and approach only the people I knew, now I do the opposite. I look for new people to connect with — which opens up opportunities and creates energy for me and for them. I know now that you have to put yourself out there to see how you can inspire better leadership in the corporate environment — it creates the energy you need to follow your passions in your personal life, too. Don't put things on the shelf because of work; all your passions drive the intrinsic value in you as a person. That's the essence of true leadership: you draw on a breadth of experience and thinking. You don't just sit in your office and work hard.

My ability to take risks was unlocked in my early twenties by a defining moment that changed everything. That dream of one day being CFO? I made it. But even better, I've since moved above and beyond.

6

Lifelong Learning

No matter how high you climb in your career, you'll still have to be able to figure out things you don't know. These can range from mastering a new skill, like basic accounting, to learning how to be a better leader. It can be a humbling experience, but lifelong learning is a very effective asset for a leader. You'll be in a better position to coach, to problem-solve with your team, to think laterally and spot important changes in the landscape that could affect your business. That's critical today, as technology solutions put all our business models at risk. You always have to be open to considering a new way of thinking about your business, and prepared to learn something new. If you don't, you're toast.

Colleen Sidford

FORMER VICE PRESIDENT AND TREASURER, CHIEF INVESTMENT OFFICER, ONTARIO POWER GENERATION INC.

Don't Wait to Boost Women

My leadership lesson began in 2008, while I was the chief investment officer at Ontario Power Generation Inc. It was at this late point in my career when I realized that the women in my own organization weren't making it to the senior positions. And after participating in The Judy Project and networking with so many successful women across Canada, I was determined to find out why.

So I conducted some informal research, which included talking with a number of other companies who were confronting a similar problem. I came to the conclusion that women just weren't being recognized as potential leaders. And it wasn't because they didn't have the requisite expertise or experience, but because they weren't projecting leadership traits — such as personal confidence, along with clarity and brevity of message, whether written or verbal. They weren't exuding a leadership presence, and as a result they were being bypassed for promotions. Meanwhile our male counterparts seemed to exhibit these traits naturally, and were recognized by the decision makers — also predominantly men.

I wanted to encourage women to learn more about leadership so that they too could find a way to connect to those leadership roles. I engaged the Humphrey Group and enlisted some of my like-minded colleagues to help me build a program around Humphrey's "Taking the Stage" program. We customized the training for our industry so that it could be adapted to women working at every level in the organization: management, technical, professional, and administrative. We added to the curriculum a component about developing a personal brand, a leadership concept borrowed from The Judy Project.

"ALTHOUGH IT'S IMPORTANT TO SEE MORE WOMEN ACHIEVE C-SUITE POSITIONS AND TO SERVE ON BOARDS, IT'S ALSO EXTREMELY IMPORTANT TO HELP WOMEN EARLIER."

—*Colleen Sidford*

And thus, after obtaining formal approval from the OPG board of directors, in the fall of 2008 we launched a pilot program called emPOWERed Women. With a focus on personal leadership skills, the first program ran over a four-month period, with 15 participants. From this modest launch, we eventually delivered four one-day sessions semiannually, providing training to more than 650 women over the next five years. Today, some of the emPOWERed Women carry on the work by continuing to hold ad hoc sessions.

This program was unusual in that it was run not by HR but by a group of passionate volunteers. After every half-year session, we hosted a graduation celebration for which each group selected a valedictorian to speak on their behalf. The graduates' managers as well as the OPG executive and board were invited to attend the ceremony; it was quite powerful and emotional for everyone. In fact, the graduates became so invested in the program's benefits that in subsequent years they volunteered to continue to keep that power of connection alive by acting as facilitators and helping train their female colleagues.

The program saw great results. We were able to track and measure its value by demonstrating that its graduates were being promoted to more senior positions at faster rates than the general employee population over the same time period. After just four months, women who had formerly been timid and unnoticed were being selected for more senior roles — and they were implementing change throughout the organization. In 2010, the emPOWERed Women program was recognized by Catalyst Canada in its first Business Champion category.

The connections I'd made at The Judy Project were my catalyst in making a major change for other women in my organization. Although it's important to see more women achieve C-suite positions and to serve on boards, it's also extremely important to pay it forward — to help women earlier, as they progress through their careers, so that they'll have the potential and confidence to achieve these important roles.

Sandy Sharman

SENIOR EXECUTIVE VICE PRESIDENT
AND CHIEF HUMAN RESOURCES
AND COMMUNICATIONS OFFICER, CIBC

Doing an MBA at Night

My decision to do my MBA part time over four years was driven by a desire to prove to myself that I had the ability to learn at a new level. I was working full time and had a family, but hey, as the old adage goes, "The busier you are, the more you get done!"

When I arrived home from the hospital with my one-day-old son, Gavin (Liam, my eldest, was five years old), the textbooks for my first class were waiting on my doorstep. I just looked at them and thought, *What in the world was I thinking?*

And so began a four-year period in which I was constantly balancing on a very thin line, prioritizing what was important while navigating a busy life with two small children, a husband who was successful in his policing career (yes, that meant shift work), and my school and work demands. I often refer to it as my "after 9:30 p.m. and before 6 a.m. MBA"! But I did it. And I was stronger for having had that challenge.

So, life is about choices. And to ensure that my choice to pursue an MBA would be a success, I needed the help of everyone around me, a support system. I like what my sister Cathy says about that: "You work your plan, and plan your work, and you *can* have it all."

It was a proud moment to walk across the stage at graduation; my three guys were there hooting and hollering and cheering me on. Because, in reality, we all did it together.

GOOD ADVICE
Navigating in a Male-Dominated Industry

My leadership lessons began well before becoming chief executive partner at Osler. I'd worked with great leaders within our firm and among our clients in my mergers and acquisitions practice, and had observed very different styles of effective and authentic leadership. But they were invariably male role models. In such a male-dominated industry, I necessarily learned a lot about navigating that world as a woman and influencing the boardrooms I found myself in. I also learned a lot about the power of generosity — so many of these leaders were generous to me.

Look to the long game. In high-performance environments, we're apt to expend all our focus and energy on the challenge immediately before us. And in my experience, women in particular can lose sight of planning for long-term success. My advice: Be strategic about planning your career. Seek out assignments that will differentiate you, challenge and energize you, and gain you recognition for leadership capacity. This in turn will build your confidence, which is an imperative. Develop your personal brand and your network. Seek out mentors at all levels. And since we disregard internal constituencies at the cost of effecting meaningful change, remember to maintain a support base within your organization, even at the later stages of leadership. Strong communication, and bringing others along with you, are vital.

Market yourself. It's easy to get focused on doing a great job and to believe that your results will speak for themselves. But as you're developing your career, you really must *package* and *market* your performance. Women often believe that recognition will follow from achieving great outcomes, that there's no need to *blow their own horn* since strong performance should be obvious for all to see. Well, the truth is, that's just not necessarily so!

—Dale Ponder

National Co-Chair,
Osler, Hoskin & Harcourt LLP

Linda MacKay

SENIOR VICE PRESIDENT, PERSONAL BANKING, DISTRIBUTION, AND STRATEGY, TD BANK

Lessons Learned

I can boil down my leadership lessons learned over a long career into five pieces of advice:

1. **"Dwell in possibility …"** That's the title of an Emily Dickinson poem I love. Most people don't know the whole poem, but many know the title as a quote in and of itself. I think it speaks to the idea Judy Elder articulated when she gave her speech on declaring your ambition and then going for it.

   Much of leadership is about believing in yourself and your potential and, even more so, the potential of others. For me, it's about helping colleagues expand the boundaries of what they believe to be their personal potential. While careers can start out by balancing your emotional quotient, your curiosity, and your intelligence, over time the intelligence piece isn't the differentiator. EQ and curiosity become the differentiators for leaders — how you relate to people; how you communicate, solve problems, and help those on your team be better and do better than they thought possible. Believing in possibility, along with helping others to see and achieve it, is a powerful leadership lesson and attribute.

2. **Be early, be honest when faced with problems.**
   When something goes wrong — and it will, often
   — my mantra is to be early and be honest. Deal with
   tough issues head on. As hard and as awkward as those
   conversations can be with your boss or colleagues, it's
   far better to solve problems quickly than let them linger
   and possibly become worse.

   Early in my career, when I made a mistake or a
   problem emerged, I'd spend a lot of time thinking
   about how to fix it. That's quite a bit of pressure for
   one person, and often the situation gets worse day by
   day. Bringing in a colleague or boss early and asking
   for help means getting to a better solution, faster. It also
   demonstrates your character, integrity, and commitment
   to doing the right thing. It ensures that you'll have
   the chance to get help before the situation becomes
   unsolvable, and takes more time and resources than it
   ever should have in the first place.

3. **Help others succeed.** Good leaders recognize that
   helping others speaks to their own leadership. You won't
   need to showcase what you've done; those around
   you will quickly make the connection that you have
   a high-performing team or are a key contributor to
   the team. And I've found that recognizing people on a
   daily basis bolsters their success, whether you give them
   a handwritten card, send a thank-you email, have an
   encouraging chat when you pass in the hallway, or say
   thanks in front of others in a meeting.

   Recently, we were going into what promised to be
   a lengthy, difficult meeting. Ahead of time, I got the

team member who'd be leading the meeting a thank-
you card and gift card. And at the end of the meeting
(which went well, as I'd thought it would), I gave her
the recognition she'd earned and deserved — in front
of the person heading up the project. Those things
mean a lot to people. Recognition and gratitude are
too important to be left as an afterthought.

4. **Stay authentic.** I have a philosophy of demonstrating
    fun and a sense of humour, especially when things are
    tense. It helps people work better together. As you reach
    senior levels in an organization, people often feel they
    can't approach you; they're intimidated by you simply
    by virtue of your position. So it's important to stay true
    to who you are.

    I also make it a priority to be transparent. Before or
    after meetings I have really honest conversations with
    folks on my team — about what I'm worried about, or
    how I think it might play out. But I get them to share
    their views, too. I encourage people to disagree with
    me. In fact, I often assign someone the role of devil's
    advocate in important meetings; I'll challenge someone
    to be the dissenter. Because we have to know how
    something can go very right, or horribly wrong, *before*
    we execute.

5. **Hire for will, train for skill.** In my business, we exist
    to help customers. Ultimately the customer is your
    paycheque, so it's important to make sure you have a
    great team that can deliver the experience the customer
    expects and deserves. To that end, I hire for will, and

train for skill. That means I put a lot of importance on hiring people with the right attitude, passion, and alignment with our values. That's critical. I'd argue that it's almost impossible to create a great attitude (or passion or values) where they don't naturally exist. People who might not necessarily tick every box in terms of qualifications are often great assets on your team because they're curious: they ask terrific questions, and they question things the rest of us might take for granted. It's easier for someone to grow in skills and competencies than it is in attitude and will.

Q&A

Dale Ponder

National Co-Chair, Osler, Hoskin & Harcourt LLP

Q. **What makes you a lifelong learner?**

A. I think lifelong learners are basically challenge seekers. They challenge themselves to be the best they can be. And I'm going to attribute the start of my appetite for challenge to one of my grade school teachers. I have a vivid recollection of Mr. Simmons, my grade four teacher in my hometown of Timmins, Ontario, taking me aside after class to criticize my performance in math. He said, "Dale, you're smart, you know how to do this, so why aren't you?" For the first time, a teacher was telling me two new things of importance: I was smart and, in fact, good at math!

In hindsight, I recognize what had been holding me back in that long-ago grade four class: a lack of confidence and, importantly, a belief that math just wasn't something girls did well. Change the fact pattern, and these are two recognizable constraints that women repeatedly impose on themselves! So I owe a huge debt of gratitude to Mr. Simmons, because this was a turning point for me.

That early experience set the stage for my education: as I proceeded in school, I took every math course as well as lots of science. I now recognize that this was about challenging myself and pursuing things that girls generally didn't. I also became hungry to be among the best at those things, and in the process, I became comfortable with men. In both friendship and competition.

I recently read a leadership study that found you either have that desire for constant challenge and actively seek it, or you don't. Well, to take the other side of this, I think we can learn to thrive on challenge. I consider challenge and a bit of adversity to be one of the absolute best opportunities for learning. My parents certainly supported my appetite for this; they instilled in me the belief that there was nothing I couldn't do if I set my mind to it. Being a girl was never part of the conversation. Despite growing up in a mining town and my parents having no formal education — they were immigrants and small-town entrepreneurs — they presumed I'd have a university education and a serious career. As a result, so did I.

Q. **So, going to law school was the career goal?**

A. No (laughing)! I started at Queen's University, planning to be a pediatrician. I was happy in first year pre-med, but in second term I was surprised to find that physics was a struggle, and that gave me a crisis of confidence. For the first time, it occurred to me that I might not make it into med school so easily. So instead of carrying on with the program, I abandoned that pursuit. I'm not proud of that decision; I consider myself to be more determined and resilient than I was at that moment.

In an about-face, I decided to transfer into — wait for it — audiology and speech pathology. One of the toughest programs to get into, but a tremendously bad move for me. Patience is not my long suit, and therapy requires buckets of that admirable quality. It wasn't long before I thought, *I'm so bored. What am I doing here?*

My unhappiness must have been palpable, because the person I was dating at the time, who planned to go into law, said to me, "You're so unhappy with school. Why don't you write the LSAT with me this weekend as a walk-in?" And I thought, *Interesting. I wonder if I'd be good at law?* So, on a whim, I wrote the LSAT — and luckily hit it out of the park. Admittedly, there was a component on neuroanatomy, which was just great good luck; it must have been meant to be.

Q. **Did learning law come easily?**

A. Well, it certainly was different. But I loved the newness of it, and as I continued my studies I found that if I chose the courses reputed to be toughest, I really would apply myself. For example, most students were a bit terror-struck by tax law — so I specialized in tax. I still really didn't know what kind of career I was pursuing; I'd never even *known* any lawyers. I just thought that if I went after the toughest courses then all would be well.

I looked at it as an adventure — an opportunity to learn and be challenged in something new and to discover whether I could excel in something beyond math and science. At the time, law school was dominated by men, and frankly, that suited me well, too. Growing up as the tomboy I'd been, I felt comfortable in that environment and with the competition in both school and sports. And school was a more even playing field for me than sports!

To begin my career I moved to Toronto to practise tax law, but it soon became clear to me that my first firm was stronger in securities law than in tax. Securities was also a very male world, with next to no women in the field — not as lawyers, investment bankers, or clients. And, funnily enough given my later career, I'd never taken a securities law course. So I set out to teach myself securities law. I worked at it in my free time. And by the end of my first year, I began practising securities law.

Q. **Just a wild guess, but it couldn't have been too long before you were looking for your next challenge!**

A. Five years into my career, Osler encountered me when I was leading the Campbell Soup IPO, representing the underwriters. Osler decided they wanted me to join them and hired a head-hunter to pursue me. They were considered a leader in securities law, but I still found the deci-sion to move a tough one, and again, nearly succumbed to a crisis of confidence.

This time I went looking for advice from a senior woman I admired from another firm. She told me, "Dale, whatever you do, don't say no because you think you're not good enough." I was reminded then of how I'd shrugged off medicine. The result was I did move firms — and for me, it's been a great decision.

I set myself the tough goal of making part-ner within a year of joining Osler. To succeed, I knew that many partners would have to know who I was and that I'd have to distinguish myself quickly, so I sought out tough assignments. And I found a big one! The deal was stunningly compli-cated, and both the client and the partner on the file were known for regularly chewing through young lawyers. In hindsight, putting my hand up for such a tough assignment was taking a big risk because it might have blown up in my face. But my experiences had taught me to never back away from challenges prematurely or dwell on the potential for bad consequences. It all turned out well, and another lesson learned.

Q. **Has your hunger for learning benefited your firm more widely?**

A. I sure hope so, since I went on to lead it! But at the time, leading the firm was a goal furthest from my mind. I enjoyed the adrenalin of mergers and acquisitions and working with clients. Although I never sought the role, I'd also regularly been engaged in leadership in a smaller context. In hindsight, my involvement in important committee work gave me the opportunity to both learn and demonstrate decision-making skills, business judgment, and leadership capacity. And in turn, it allowed my partners to get a strong sense of my values and priorities.

These were the experiences that led to a role of co–managing partner, and then national managing partner and chief executive. And why did I agree to such a big change? Well, it was an opportunity to make a difference. And I thought, *That's a challenge, and definitely one great, steep learning curve.*

I became chief executive partner in 2009, at the onset of the Great Recession. Not auspicious timing, but the adage "Let no crisis go unused" resonated. The economic crash allowed me the opportunity to accelerate change and pursue a far more sophisticated business model. We've not stopped as a firm, and I can safely say that we've now embraced change; innovation is the foremost priority for us.

Q. **Now that you've accomplished so much, has that desire to learn started to wane?**

A. Well, my passionately held view is that if you're not still learning and challenging yourself, you're not fully engaged in life. A challenge is always going to be what gets me up in the morning. So don't hang up your skates too early — because you'll surely regret it!

Carol McNamara

SENIOR VICE PRESIDENT,
COMPENSATION & BENEFITS, RBC

Know Your Strengths

As I reflect on my leadership experience, one of the principles that have guided me through a fulfilling career journey is staying focused on my strengths. At stages during my career, I've felt uncertain in my ability to master the skills needed for new assignments or roles. And it's in those times of self-doubt that I've needed to stay especially focused on my strengths — which are invariably character traits rather than technical knowledge.

The proof point for me was when I found myself on a steep learning curve after being appointed to a new and rewarding role in human resources, following 30 years in legal roles. Newly responsible for overseeing compensation, pension, and benefits for our global company, I felt I had to focus on my knowledge gaps, in particular the accounting implications of our HR programs.

So I enrolled in a night course in accounting — a humbling experience when my exam results came in! But as a result of that effort, I learned that I should focus on what I'm good at, including the strategic and leadership aspects of human resources, and rely on the experts around me for what I'm missing.

LETTER TO MY DAUGHTER

Jane Russell
Executive Vice President, TD Bank

Dear Kiera,

You're still only nine years old. But when I think about your future, there are so many things that I wish for you: a life of health and happiness, fun and laughter, strength and support from great friends, colleagues, and family, and a career that inspires and motivates you.

I'm sure your personality, determination, sense of humour, innate curiosity, and clever nature will serve you well in whatever you do. But I'd like to offer a little guidance. While I'm not someone who dwells on the past, hindsight can be the best kind of wisdom. I've learned many lessons over my career — lessons I hope will help you when you embark on your own journey. And though you may not want to hear it now, I hope this advice will come in handy in a few years.

Be decisive, but not inflexible. This is the most important leadership lesson I can share. The ability to make a decision quickly and confidently is a trait that I appreciate in other leaders, and it has helped me succeed and grow as a manager and a leader. I've had to make many decisions — sometimes difficult or unpopular ones — but I don't hesitate to voice my opinion and decide. To do that, I use my judgment and rely on my professional experience to guide me so that I don't waver or hesitate.

But you have to know the difference between acting with conviction and just being stubborn. If additional information becomes available, if the landscape, environment, or facts change, be flexible and willing to revisit your decision — whether you made it a month ago or even a year ago. And if you refuse to take other factors into consideration, if you're rigid and unwilling to yield, that's being obstinate, not purposeful.

Take chances. Relocating for new jobs is something I've done a few times. I started out working in Toronto, relocated to western Canada, where you were born, and returned to Toronto. A couple of years ago, when I was the head of our mortgage business in Canada, I was asked to take on a new role in New Jersey. The easier choice would have been to stay put: our lives, routines, friends, and extended family were in the Toronto area. And I knew I didn't want to travel back and forth, working in the U.S. during the week and going home for weekends. But I was up for the challenge. So we pulled up roots again and moved here, ready for another adventure.

The new role was challenging in many ways. For one thing, the competition in this industry in the United States is extraordinary. Plus, I've had to learn how we do business in the U.S., how to best engage with customers, and how to handle the regulatory environment. On top of it all, most of my new colleagues didn't know me, and I didn't know them.

However, my desire to learn quickly proved to be valuable, and it paid off. In 2017 and 2018 I was honoured by *American Banker* as one of the "Women to Watch" in the industry (and in 2017, was even featured with eight other women on the cover!).

The move has been an adventure for all of us. I'm so glad you quickly made friends in your new school and have learned to play field hockey and lacrosse. We've travelled and explored here together, and we've seen and experienced so many things. It's been remarkable and rewarding for your dad and me to see you enjoying everything.

If I hadn't pushed out of my comfort zone and made it a point to seek out other opportunities, we might all have missed out on so many amazing things. So be open, be willing to get a little uncomfortable, and you too will find inspiration.

Never stop learning. TD Bank is the only company I've ever worked for; it's been 30 years. These days, staying with one company is becoming more and more unusual. Most people have different jobs at different companies, and I suspect you will, too. But I've stayed here for so long because I've continued to learn, at every stage and in every role. I've moved into different parts of the organization, each time having a better opportunity — and I don't mean only professionally.

So I say, keep learning. Challenge yourself, ask questions, be curious, and always live in the moment. When you have knowledge, you're ready for any opportunity that comes your way. My career has had its fair share of twists and turns, so don't simply focus on getting from point A to point B, but on the experiences in between. If you aren't learning and enjoying the ride, reconsider your path.

I hope you take many chances in life, and find your path. I hope you always look around, stay energized and inspired, and keep your sense of excitement. I hope you dream big and think outside the box, but still remember to find joy along the way. I know you'll do amazing things!

Love,
Mamma

7

Tenacity

Tenacity is an excellent leadership muscle, one that needs to be developed, especially in ambitious female leaders. It gives you perspective when you hit short-term challenges on your way to achieving a long-term goal. It helps you to stay the course when corporate life is hard.

And it may well be hard. You might find you've been moved sideways in a corporate reorganization or sideswiped by a disaster at home. You'll probably encounter unconscious bias, the invisible rules that can hold women back. They often present hurdles that your male peers don't have to deal with. Your leadership strengths may be less traditional and therefore may not be as recognized or appreciated. You may be less vocal than your male counterparts. Your organization may assume that certain roles are for men and others are for women. These invisible rules even appear at home, when it's assumed, for example, that women ought to take the full parental leave rather than share it with their spouses.

Business success is often a ground war, and in this game, you'll win one foot at a time. As Alison Coville describes in this chapter's first story, corporate success comes by playing the long game!

A tenacious leader overcomes. She is always, relentlessly there. She never gives up.

Alison Coville

FORMER PRESIDENT, HUDSON'S BAY

Moving Sideways in a Corporate Reorganization

My cell phone was pressed to my ear as I paced my bedroom one evening in 2012. Richard Baker — the owner of Hudson Bay Company, my boss's boss, someone I truly respected — was trying to help me gain some perspective on a move he wanted me to make within the company. "You feel I'm a good leader, right?" he said. "Yes, of course," I responded. "Okay then," he said. "Sometimes you have to hitch your wagon to successful people, trust that you too will be successful, and take the job that's there."

My mind whirled. In an environment where a lot of people were being let go, that morning I'd been offered a senior VP position outside of the retail roles I'd typically worked in. I was already an SVP, and I'd had my sights set higher; it felt like my results were now being overlooked. My whole career, most of which I'd spent with the Bay, had been focused on fashion. Not only did the offer not feel like a good fit, it wasn't what I wanted to do. So when I was told about it at work earlier that day, I was angry, and pushed back. I went to HR and asked them what my options were for leaving the company. Then I went home, calling my husband to tell him the news and to vent.

Now I was trying to make sense of what Richard was telling me on the phone: "We could have let you go. That would have been easy. But we need you in this position because it's right for the company. Take some time and think about it."

In the coming days I struggled with the decision, wondering if this was my time to move on. Then my daughter, who was 12, helped put things in perspective. "Let me get this straight," she said. "They're not taking any money away from you. You'll still be a senior VP. And your job won't be as crazy. Why are you upset?" The magnitude of the ego that was in the way dawned on me. So, ultimately, I did what I always told my kids to do: Put on my big-girl pants and get on with it.

It was the best decision I've ever made. I was in the role for a year, and had so much fun. I subsequently took on positions I'd been passed over for in the first place. Plus, the experience was great preparation for a role I took on for three years starting in 2014: SVP and managing director of Hudson's Bay Home and Home Outfitters.

Once again, the role was unexpected, and something that wasn't in my wheelhouse; never had I imagined that I'd run such a large — and, frankly, tired — home business in 90 Bay locations, plus the Home Outfitters chain. But this time, right from the start, I embraced the change, and the challenge, wholly.

Globally, the market was becoming a major growth category; the customer wanted to spend money on her home and on entertaining. Yet, overall, our business wasn't inspirational or contemporary enough. For example, we were overinvested in areas like fine china while the market was moving to casual dining. Our bedding and bath assortments were too basic while specialty stores were selling colour and whimsy. We treated our cookware as functional instead of the sexy product it could be to shoppers who were now foodies and coffee aficionados.

Clearly, we required major product re-engineering and a new marketing image. So I looked at how we could elevate the product. With the support of the creative director for home, we worked to reinvent key categories, starting with a brand we owned called Distinctly Home. We crafted a brand essence that was fun, modern, and affordable. We designed bedding and towels and accessories that made it easy, and affordable, to decorate. We changed the branding and graphics on packaging and in our stores to reflect the new image — and we did it quickly. It was exciting stuff.

The corporate strategy at the time was to decrease the number of home-oriented products in stores (or, in some stores, to exit the home category altogether) in order to grow other businesses like fashion. This could have discouraged the teams, but I rallied them with the mantra "We are shrinking ourselves to greatness!" I wanted them to be on the offence versus the defence. "Don't think of this as something that's happening *to* you," I told them. "Instead, own it."

We made decisions to have fewer products, but great ones. And we wanted less duplication; we didn't need five gadget brands — just two that were new. We jumped on trends. For example, one of our buyers quickly addressed the coffee craze, sourcing all the newest machines and emerging technologies. The result? We became known as a destination for coffee connoisseurs. In other words, we needed to do the edit for the customer — to create the clarity so that she wouldn't have to. I led a new mindset: *We* were the experts, so let's deliver more unique and exciting products.

And, importantly, I realized that I was in a good position for this transformation not despite but because of my fashion background. I applied my knowledge of fashion to the home business: What's the next big trend? What brands are emerging as unique and exciting? What are the colours of the season that we can add to towels to freshen up our customers' "home wardrobe"?

Meanwhile, many changes needed to be made behind the scenes, too: things like operating processes and a consistent tracking of results. We looked at the talent and made changes if needed. Everyone from management to the associates on the floor had to have the same passion for elevated products. We got lots of momentum, and our home business grew dramatically the following year. Profits soared. Over two years, a major segment of our bedding and bath products grew by 24 percent while sales of overall home products grew 11 percent. And these results created huge momentum: the teams have had year-over-year growth every season since!

I learned a lot about being a leader in the years since I ended up accepting the position that, at first, I didn't feel was right. Now I tell others that when an opportunity comes along, whether you think it's a good fit for you or not, consider taking it for the sake of learning something valuable. And remember that nothing ever stays the same.

Paula Hodgins

PRESIDENT, HEWLETT PACKARD ENTERPRISE CANADA

When Your Marriage Ends, the Inner Fighter Comes Out

The year my first child turned one, my marriage ended. I was devastated. And since I was living in the U.S. at the time, I had no family support. I was at the lowest point I'd ever been in my life. So I knew I had to decide: I could be a victim, or I could take control of my future and make it great for myself and my young son.

As a woman working in the world of technology, I'd spent most of my career in a male-dominated culture, with few female role models. I'd sought out male and female sponsors and mentors who could help me navigate, but ultimately I found that the key to success is having the ability to believe in myself, and being very determined not to let anyone steal my dreams.

So I gathered up my inner fighter, and this propelled me forward. I moved back to Vancouver with my son and started a new job, hiring a nanny for extra support while I worked. I began to put the pieces of my life back together.

It is this tenacity from that time in my life that has helped me to overcome adversity in the years since, to not shy away from tough challenges or things I'm afraid to do — because I know I can figure them out. In fact, after this experience, every challenge I face, while not easy, does remind me that I have it within me to figure things out.

I'm lucky to have learned this valuable lesson relatively early. My experience taught me that tenacity and resilience aren't qualities you can pull out of a hat when you need them. You have to work on building them in yourself every day, so that the muscle is strong when you need to lean on it.

I've faced many complex, challenging situations in my career over the years. Many of them have been difficult and even downright scary. Having the courage to face these situations while remaining undaunted — not intimidated or discouraged by difficulty — is a muscle I've been working hard to strengthen. It's something that has carried me through my career.

It's amazing how an adverse life event and even day-to-day challenges can become the best experiences, because they help you grow the most.

Helena Gottschling

CHIEF HUMAN RESOURCES OFFICER, RBC

New City, New Role

In 2004, after having spent my entire career in western Canada, I was transferred to Toronto. Not only was this an entirely new city, it was an entirely new role, very different from what I'd done until that point. Since the bank was going through a major restructuring, it was also a time of significant change. And during this transition, my husband and son stayed out West for three months.

The job was challenging. I'd never been in a strategy role before, and outside of the support from some colleagues, I felt alone. I was coming into an environment of well-established networks and a great deal of history. There were a number of things on my mind — potentially failing in the role, not being able to adapt to the head-of-fice culture, having to form new relationships. But I also had resolve.

I knew I could do the job. Not only was I writing my own mandate and determining the resources I needed to deliver, I was learning as much as possible on the go. I was also very deliberate when building my team, staffing roles with people who had skills that I didn't. And with my family still in Calgary, I spent the extra time I needed to prepare for the days and weeks ahead, all the while travelling back and forth to spend time with my husband and son on weekends.

I made the decision that failure was not an option. I had the capabilities to succeed, and had been tested in previous roles. This was definitely different, and I had to adapt my approach, but I knew that being uncomfortable meant that I was growing and learning. It was challenging. I had to dig deep at times. But being focused and tenacious on overcoming one challenge at a time — along with some very supportive colleagues — helped me to be successful.

Q&A

Tracy Sandler
Partner, Osler, Hoskin & Harcourt LLP

Q. **Getting to the level of partner at a major law firm has to be tough. Are there particular challenges for women?**

A. I've been fortunate at Osler. The firm and the partners in the years I was developing my practice were very supportive of women, and of me. There weren't many women in my area of law, and few women role models. The restructuring partners, led by Gordon Marantz in the early 1990s, were all men. But they were strongly of the view that family came first, and they led by example. If one of my children was sick, they encouraged me to focus on my child.

While they expected 100 percent commitment and unwavering excellence, they taught me to balance all aspects of my life. I was also taught to delegate up, to be fierce, to find my voice and be independent, and to be a leader. I can comfortably command a room. And since

I'm five feet tall on a good day, with my ballet posture, I always wear high heels to provide added authority!

My parents' outlook also made me feel I could achieve anything. My sister and I were expected to work hard, set goals, and then reach them — and more. My dad had lived through World War II in London, during the Blitz. So whenever we complained about noise in the house while we were trying to study, he would remind us that he got his engineering degree by studying in a bomb shelter with 50 of his neighbours.

My biggest challenge in reaching partnership was with myself. In order to really find my voice, I needed to be courageous, and to accept that I wasn't always going to be perfect. Some days I'd be a better mom than a lawyer, or vice versa. You need to forgive yourself for that and move on.

I learned to juggle, to compartmentalize, and to laugh. My first day of work after my second maternity leave, I was feeling like I had it all under control — until I looked at my suit while in a meeting and saw that it was covered in blue sparkle paint. I rocked that meeting.

Q. **Besides drive, sometimes in law you need a salesperson's mindset, right?**

A. Definitely you do in my area, insolvency and restructuring. As you can imagine, we don't often have repeat clients in this business, so you have to build your reputation, get out in the market, and find the next case. It takes perseverance and some chutzpah.

Our practice group had the vision to understand that the big restructuring opportunities were in the U.S. market. Gordon Marantz called me into his office one day to say that he wanted me to start marketing in New York, Boston, and Chicago — wherever it took. I was to build my brand in the U.S. and develop a market presence there. Advising me that he was going to alert his American friends, he picked up the phone and said, "I'm sending my girl down."

I'm really grateful that he had such confidence in me. Of course, I didn't know anyone and was mildly terrified. I went alone, and would literally find these guys at some huge cocktail reception, march up to them, flash my trademark Sandler grin, and introduce myself: "Hi, I'm Tracy Sandler, from Osler in Toronto." I learned to create new relationships from scratch, and many of these business relationships became personal friends. I'm often introduced by U.S. colleagues as the Queen of Canada. Our group is held out within the firm as the model for business development.

Q. **Creating those new relationships takes tenacity.**

A. Well, that was nothing compared to one of the first assignments I was given. It's burned on my brain. I was 23, and had to go see a client I'd never met, someone who was selling personal assets to get out of some financial difficulty. He was unhappy about his situation and took it out on me. When I walked into his office to have him sign the papers, he had a massive cigar going and an enormous glass of scotch. He was huge, he was drunk, he was very abusive — and he was unwilling to sign. I didn't know what to do other than gamely try to persuade him to sign so that I could make a graceful exit. He kept telling me I was incompetent. Finally, I persuaded him to call the partner. He did, advising him that he hoped Osler had liability insurance for me. The partner laughed and got him to sign.

I made my exit, and only then did I cry — out of rage because I was young, it was my first deal, and I hadn't known how to respond in that situation. The client was physically intimidating, and I'd felt unsafe. That was a defining moment. I knew I'd never let myself get into circumstances again that I couldn't control.

THE MOMENT

That was a defining moment. I knew I'd never let myself get into circumstances again that I couldn't control.

Q. **Have you had to handle tense situations since?**

A. Insolvency is a crisis practice, with many tense moments. Our clients are often fighting for their corporate lives. We see people in the most stressful situations of their business lives and sometimes their personal lives. For example, I led Target's exit from Canada. Almost 20,000 people lost their jobs on the first day of the case. It was very difficult. Over time, I've learned that I can be the calm at the centre of the storm. I don't run from chaos and crisis; I've learned to thrive in it — to take control and build consensus to drive a resolution.

Q. **Is there a trick to that?**

A. I do it in part by focusing on developing personal relationships. I also try to use humour to defuse stressful moments. You have to build trust among the key players. In working with a new client team, I very quickly focus on the personal. In some ways I'm actually more interested in the people aspect of my job, because that's what makes the work so interesting. We're in the trenches for long periods of time. Many of my clients have become very close personal friends. I've seen them go through divorces, new careers, second families.

To manage stress, I'm also a firm believer in exercise. I run, do cross training, and see a personal trainer three times a week. I go to yoga class once a week. My yoga teacher is forcing me to practise sitting still. We're up to 30 seconds: now *that* is stressful!

Shelly Lazarus

CHAIRMAN EMERITUS, OGILVY & MATHER

We've Come a Long Way, Baby

When I first started my career in the 1970s, it was perfectly acceptable in the United States for a prospective employer to say the following things to a woman:

- "We'd love to give you a job, but part of the training program involves three months in the sales force, and it's so heavy taking the sample case in and out of the car."

- "We'd love to give you a job, but what would our account executives' wives say when you had to work late with their husbands?"

- "We'd love to give you a job, but there are so few spots, and we couldn't waste one on a woman."

These were all things that were *actually* said to me in 1970 by representatives of companies that are revered and honoured today. I won't tell you who they were.

But I'll also never forget!

Women have made progress on pay equality. And yet we're all impatient. What's taking so long? I actually think impatience is a good thing. It applies pressure. It makes things happen. But while advocating impatience, I also think it's important to maintain perspective, and recognize how far our efforts have taken us.

GOOD ADVICE
Inspiration from Maya Angelou

When my daughter, Rachel, was 21, she got an internship at a global corporation. In preparation for this role, she asked me for some advice on navigating the professional world and creating her own brand. I know from personal experience that this task requires tenacity, and I shared with her some quotes I've taken with me from Maya Angelou, the late American poet and civil rights advocate. I find these mantras to be not only helpful for a young woman starting out, but also incredibly applicable at any career stage.

"If you don't like something, change it. If you can't change it, change your attitude."
Work and life throw many challenges at you. To make these obstacles work *for* you, it's important to be proactive about creating meaningful change and being flexible enough to adjust your mentality to progress forward when change is out of your control.

"I've learned that you shouldn't go through life with a catcher's mitt on both hands; you need to be able to throw something back."
Engage in the questions and issues around you; don't just sit back and absorb information. Take every opportunity to participate in meetings, ask questions, and contribute meaningful ideas to drive growth. A willingness to take part in the action demonstrates the importance of your presence to others and allows you to create ownership.

"I learned a long time ago the wisest thing I can do is be on my own side, be an advocate for myself and others like me."

Ultimately, you are your own woman. You possess authorship of your personal brand, so take opportunities to advocate for yourself and your team through each project, interaction, and collaboration. Be confident in your abilities and in what you can bring to the table. At that table, never be afraid to take the head seat. Finally, remember that we all play a role in advocating for and supporting the next generation of women leaders.

—Rowena Chan
Senior Vice President, Sun Life

Martine Irman

VICE CHAIR, TD SECURITIES;
SENIOR VICE PRESIDENT, TD BANK GROUP

"Get Out There and Prove Them Wrong!"

Picture this: It's the late 1990s, and I'm running a TD Securities business called Global Money Markets. I get a call from my boss, the CEO: "Martine, I'm going to make some changes. We're going to merge some of our business lines into one, and I want you to lead it." Just like that, my two colleagues, both men, were no longer on the same level as me; one was being let go, and the other would now report to me. I had not seen the promotion coming. It was pretty exciting.

Right after the announcement, I walked onto the trading floor. It was midday. International markets like Singapore, London, Sydney, and Hong Kong were all mic'd in, and internal cameras on our floor were running so that the other offices could see me.

Never been on a trading floor? I can describe it as a gigantic classroom where some 600 traders are sitting at rows and rows of desks. Each desk has its own computer, and overhead there are giant screens with tickers showing up-to-the-moment market activity. People are yelling and hollering into phones and at each other. It's an environment I normally feel very comfortable in.

However, this wasn't a normal day. Because when I walked in, there was only silence. I looked up at the screens, which would normally be showing stock indices like the Dow Jones, TSX, Nasdaq, LIBOR, and Currencies. All I could see was something called the MMI Index flashing "3 month bid/6 months offered." I turned to a junior trader and asked, "What is this MMI Index?"

"Well," he said (for all the offices to hear), "that's the bidding on how long the new boss will last. Basically, those numbers indicate how many months until they're fired."

I looked back up at the screen, and it dawned on me. "MMI" stood for my name, Martine Marlyse Irman. You could have heard a pin drop. Traders picked up their phones, pretending to be on them, but remaining silent and staring at me as I processed this.

I took a deep breath and then addressed the entire floor. "Okay, I want to know who's bidding three months and who's offering six months by the end of this week. If you don't come talk to me about what's working well and what isn't, you won't be around anymore. And in the next three months I want to hear — this is mandatory — from all managing directors. My door will be open to anyone for the entire three months. And I can guarantee all of you: I'll still be here in six months!"

With that, I stormed out of the trading room. Which was awkward, because my office was *in* the trading room. So where did I end up going? The women's washroom! And what did I do? Called my mother (who, by the way, had no idea what I did for a living; she thought I was an overpaid telephone operator).

"Mom, I just got this huge promotion and everyone thinks I'm going to fail."

"Oh, it's all in your head, dear," Mom said.

"Actually, it's on screens all over the world, in all our global offices."

"Well, what are you doing now?"

"Talking to you from the women's washroom!"

"Well, get out there and prove them wrong!"

The next day, as I walked back onto the trading floor, I had an epiphany when one of the chief traders pulled me aside. "You know," he said, "the MMI Index thing yesterday … It wasn't about *you*, nor about your being a woman. It was just a bit of fun. It was a way for everyone to relieve stress, and we would have done that to whoever got the mandate."

That was a pivotal lesson. He was right (and by the way, he went on to work with me for the next 15 years). Because the moral of this story is this: Get over yourself. Be a leader. You got the promotion because you deserved it. You weren't chosen so that you'd fail.

People did take me up on my offer to come talk, and I listened to them all. This empowered them. My boss hadn't set me up for failure, but rather for success; he wanted to stretch me, and he certainly achieved that.

Twenty years later, I'm still with TD. I overcame those initial insecurities. I got over myself. And from that point on, I "owned" my career. Own yours, and enjoy it along the way. It's a journey, not a destination. Bring others along.

Q&A

Annette Verschuren
Chair and CEO, NRStor Inc.

Q. **How do you see today's contentious environment of men versus women?**

A. In my over 40-year career in business I've never experienced such a vocal and visceral response to an initiative — partly fuelled by the multitude of sexual harassment allegations. Women are seeking equality in their families, careers, relationships, and communities. I've not seen a confidence and resolve like this. And I think it's just the beginning.

Q. **What are the positive results you hope will come out of it?**

A. In business I see such great economic benefits from women's increased participation in all fields. I see that boards and companies focus more on ensuring that women are promoted with fewer unconscious biases, and that they've added focused development plans. It's like mental health: the topic was avoided for a long time, but now people are more open about it. Talking, and taking action, is what we need now.

Q. In your experience as a leader of large businesses, how do men typically see you as a woman leader? And was it different a couple of decades ago?

A. Unconscious biases are still there, even at this mature time in my career. I remember walking through our Home Depot stores when I was president in the early 2000s. If a customer heard that the company president was in the store, they would always walk up to a male colleague and assume *he* was president. Our employees eventually recognized this and began adding that "she" was in the building.

Q. What's your advice to women for how to handle perceived discrimination in the workplace?

A. Be confident, and address things directly where you can. Seek advice from others. Disclose issues early — don't wait. And: Be direct.

Q. If men are worried about how to work with women in the current climate, is there a danger that this could perhaps result in fewer women being hired?

A. I have great faith that men and women will find it easier to work together. Talking about it openly will make it easier. Yes, there will be some pushback, but I believe that, overall, things will improve in our relationships.

Monique Allen

EXECUTIVE VICE PRESIDENT, ONTARIO MUNICIPAL EMPLOYEES
RETIREMENT SYSTEM

The Trap of Unconscious Bias

When my stepdaughter, Lauren, was five, she looked up at me from her breakfast one morning, curious brown eyes, hair in pigtails, and said, "Monique, tell me about God."

You're never really prepared for those delicate questions, are you? I took a few minutes to think before answering. I wanted to leave enough space in my answer that Lauren could start to form her own beliefs and ensure they left room for accepting different forms of God. I kept my response simple, focusing on values and unyielding love for everyone. She seemed to accept my answer, paused thoughtfully, and then responded, "Hmm, I wonder what She looks like."

My jaw dropped. Naturally! Why wouldn't she think God could be a woman? At five she hadn't yet been conditioned by the world around her to think anything different. She had no biases, conscious or unconscious. I found myself in a moment where I was immensely proud of this little girl's thinking and optimistic for the life she had ahead of her. I saw a little girl who had a world of opportunity in which she might not be constrained by gender stereotypes and the biases of generations before.

For years that moment stuck with me. I started to see my world differently. As I walked the floor at the office, as I sat in meetings, I saw a generation of young women and young men for whom I might be making a difference. A generation who might not feel constrained by which parent took parental leave or how they shared it between them. A generation of young minds who collaborated around the table equally and accepted each other as leaders. A generation where young women might not have to adopt masculine attributes to be accepted as leaders.

I myself was part of a mostly female technology leadership team led by a female CIO. I was proud of the changes it felt like we were making and excited about the future we were building so that girls and young women wouldn't hesitate to think they were equally suited for a variety of roles. A future where it would be only natural for them to see a woman in a leadership role — as a boss, a CEO, a prime minister, a president.

But my excitement about the progress we're making was dampened recently, and I realized that we still have a long way to go before we reinvent our mindset and eliminate unconscious bias. I had the opportunity to participate in an unconscious bias workshop, and among a group of senior leaders, of whom less than 10 percent were women, the aggregate outcome showed a strong male bias.

Perhaps I shouldn't find that outcome so unusual among my peers. Bias is a product of our environment, after all, and there's no denying that while so much positive change has occurred, we were raised in a time when many professions were dominated by men and it was unusual to see women in leadership roles. It's the awareness of unconscious bias that's most important: we can catch ourselves in those default patterns and challenge our perceptions, our decisions, the way we communicate, and the standards to which we hold others. We must continue to purposefully shape and reinvent the environment we're building for the leaders who will follow in our footsteps. We need to be deliberate about creating a world of opportunity.

It's equally important to me at home that both my stepson and stepdaughter see men and women with equal potential. So imagine my surprise one evening when I got caught in my own gender bias trip-up. My husband, Scott, and I were reflecting on a recent airline incident in which the pilot was forced to make an emergency landing. "He must have had to rely on his instruments," I remarked. Scott gave me that same look his kids give me when I've just said something that doesn't make sense, and he replied, "The pilot was a woman."

Ouch. Me, a champion of breaking gender stereotypes! Despite all the sponsorship I bring and the values I support, we're all fighting the unconscious bias that our world still reinforces around us.

I decided to test how Lauren, now 13, would react to the same story. At the dinner table I recounted the pilot story, and asked her what she thought about the pilot's situation. She paused and said, "It's a good thing he had the training to be able to react like that." Here we were, eight years later, sitting at the very same table, Lauren's pigtails now exchanged for a braid trailing down the length of her back, and this young lady fell into the very same unconscious bias trap I had.

After I told Lauren I'd made the same wrong assumption about the pilot's gender, we looked at each other and nodded with a silent understanding. Yes, we've come a long way, but there's still work to do, and influence to be made, to continue challenging our assumptions and reinventing the perception of the roles women can hold.

Sharon MacLeod

VICE PRESIDENT, GLOBAL DOVE MEN+CARE, UNILEVER

Unconscious Bias at Home

Why do so many people assume that the only parents who should take time off to care for their babies in the first year of life are women? Why shouldn't men get to stay at home with the kids in that first year, too?

In Canada, men are allowed to share parental leave with their spouses, but the uptake is small: only 15 percent of men across the country take paternity leave. One big reason is outdated masculine stereotypes that are holding men back.

Research shows that men and women have the same physiological response to taking care of young children. When men cuddle a baby, they feel the same delighted response that women do. What's more, when men take paternity leave, even for a month or so, there are all kinds of benefits — for the man, for the baby, and for the woman returning to work. Let's start with the child. Research suggests that when a father takes paternity leave, children do better emotionally and cognitively. It's called "the father effect."

The mother does better, too. Now she can focus on her career and avoid the disappointment so many women feel as they watch male colleagues surge ahead while they're at home for a year or so. Then, when the father returns to work, the couple can split tasks, which reduces the mental load of organizing birthday parties during a key planning meeting at work. It sets a pattern of behaviour that lasts a lifetime. Paternity leave may, in fact, be the most underrated way for women to be more effective at work.

Let's not forget the benefit for companies. They get to keep high-performing women at work instead of losing them.

So how can we get more men to take paternity leave? First, women need to encourage their partners to take it. Grandparents, who heavily influence the paternity decision, need to support their sons in staying at home for a few months with their children.

Many men don't know where to start. At Dove.com, where we've launched a worldwide campaign to promote paternity leave, we've put some helpful advice on our site for men who are thinking about the big ask. That would be a good thing. If more men take paternity leave, they'll be more sympathetic about the challenges women have always faced in juggling work and parental duties. Don't you think it's time?

8

Reinvention

*R*einvention may be more of a career skill than a leadership attribute. Most CEOs have led more than one business. They're well rounded, with diverse operational and geographic experiences. As you consider building your career trajectory, reinventing your skills and leadership in new and unknown roles is part of building your pedigree. It could even mean taking your skills outside the company to launch a new entrepreneurial venture.

Reinventing yourself takes courage and confidence — and frankly, women are no better at it than men are. If we step out of our job for a time to raise a family, or seek to re-enter after losing a job in a corporate restructuring, we typically look to replace our past role with the same one at a competitor. That's understandable. But why not jump at the chance to use your skills in a different way? Why not imagine the world you want to live in, and think of the work you can do there?

This means nothing short of reimagining yourself. It's profound work, so the first thing you need to do is stop and think. Instead of immediately updating your LinkedIn profile and making lunch reservations to push for a job just like your old one, envision how you want to live and what you want to do. Consider your experience, talents, relationships, aspirations, and dreams. Be ambitious!

Natasha Pekelis

MANAGING DIRECTOR, HEAD OF GLOBAL MARKETS,
IT, & QUANTITATIVE ANALYTICS, TD SECURITIES

Reinventing Yourself a Long Way from Home

I hadn't dropped onto Earth from another planet, but I might as well have. It was 1989, and I'd just landed in New York on an American Airlines flight from what was then Leningrad in the Soviet Union, now St. Petersburg in Russia. Perestroika, or the reformation of the Communist Party, had started by then and the Iron Curtain was slowly lifting. But my birthplace, the country I'd just left forever — refugees were made to give up their Russian passport and citizenship, and couldn't return — still had a palette of greys.

So America was truly a shock to the senses. I watched as a little girl put a coin into the slot at the top of a clear glass box filled with colourful candies, and one of the candies popped out into a small bowl at the bottom. I was 21, and I couldn't believe my eyes. I'd never seen a candy machine before. Nor had I ever seen so much colour, including the advertisements for fashion and cigarettes I walked past in JFK airport's wide hallways — everything was so bright!

Yet there were many conflicting emotions in my heart, the freshest being the sadness I'd felt only hours before when I'd gone through Immigration at Leningrad's Pulkovo airport. It was the point of no return, literally; I knew that the last time I'd likely ever see my family — my parents, brothers, cousins — was that glimpse of them, waving and in tears, behind the wall of glass that separated us as I walked toward my departure gate. That was tough. But I knew I had to do this if I wanted to create a new life for myself.

Why? Because of one day during my third year of studying applied mathematics at university. I was sitting near the back of a large lecture hall, listening to a philosophy professor, when he began to make false, disparaging remarks against Jewish people. I stood up and loudly told him that what he was saying wasn't true. "How do you know?" he replied. "Because I'm Jewish." I was one of the only Jewish persons to have ever been accepted to that university, so my statement surprised everyone. Hundreds of heads swivelled to stare at me. There was only silence. Finally I fled the lecture hall in tears.

At home, I told my father about it and asked him what I should do. "That's terrible, Natasha," he said. "But that's just the way it is in this country. There's nothing you can do. You'll have to accept it."

No, I didn't have to accept it. I knew it was wrong. So I made up my mind that there had to be a better place than this.

THE MOMENT

My father said, "But that's just the way it is in this country. There's nothing you can do. You'll have to accept it." I knew it was wrong. So I made up my mind that there had to be a better place than this.

At JFK, friends of my parents picked me up in a big dark-blue Buick to take me to their home, where I was to live until I got a job and a bit of money. I had $132 to my name, tucked away in my wallet. I grew excited as I realized that the stories I'd heard back in Russia about the U.S.A. seemed to be untrue. Very little outside information filtered into my home country back then. We were even told that many Americans had to live in cardboard boxes on the street. But looking around, it seemed to me that most people had a place to live.

Fast-forward to today, where I have a senior role at a multinational bank. I worked hard to reach this position: first cleaning houses, then selling sandwiches in a shop. When I got some money together, I studied at Columbia University and got a degree in computer science. That was yet another challenge, as my English was not that great. I remember studying English by listening to lessons on a Sony Walkman. I ended up graduating at the top of my class.

Thanks to everything I went through to invent a new life for myself, I gained a very good perspective on never giving up. That you always need to take the struggle to the next level, because something good will come out of it. Even when you start at a lower baseline than everyone else, you can still persevere. It helps to have a positive outlook.

I always encourage my team to take risks, especially the younger team members. To not let being at a disadvantage deter them. To try something they've never tried before. For me, that something was stepping into the complete unknown … getting onto a plane with the full understanding I'd never again go home or see my family.

My story of creating a new life has certainly had an impact on my two daughters. One is in university, and the other is still in high school. I'm so proud that they've both chosen to study science and technology and want to have careers as professionals.

Everyone has a different story and background, but the bottom line is that younger women need to have role models who inspire them to join the workforce and who nurture their careers. Young women need to know they can make for themselves a life that offers fulfillment in their work in addition to being a wife, a mother, and a member of their community.

Shauna Emerson-O'Neill

VICE PRESIDENT AND PRACTICE LEAD, STRATEGY AND
TRANSFORMATION SERVICES, RBC

Starting Over with a New Adventure

In the fall of 2015 I was riding high at Aimia Inc., the global loyalty management company. As the only female senior vice president on the executive team, I had just delivered the largest partnership transaction in our company's history. Then my corporate life suddenly changed.

There was a global restructuring, and the scope of our Canadian business was drastically reduced. My role was no exception. After 11 years of investing my all to build the business, it was clear that it was time to leave. It was a surreal situation to absorb.

Fortunately, RBC was looking for a new leader to expand its internal consulting practice, one that served senior executives across all facets of the bank. I knew about consulting, having spent the first chapter of my career as a management consultant in a top firm. Yet the opportunity felt foreign.

At Aimia I was one of the most senior leaders of a mid-sized loyalty marketing company, but if I moved to RBC, I'd be one of hundreds of executives at a huge bank. And despite having worked closely with banks throughout my career at Aimia, it was clear that I didn't have direct banking experience. In other words, after 22 years spent building my career, I'd be essentially starting over.

I'd have to rebuild my credibility in a new environment. It was an incredibly unsettling feeling.

I thought hard about whether or not I was setting myself up for success, and how difficult it might be to establish myself as a new and credible leader, given the deeply established corporate culture at the bank.

Then I thought about the themes that had fuelled my leadership style to date. I'd always been passionate about creating a tangible impact in the business. I'd focused on building trusting relationships with senior executives and on building high-performance teams. I liked to take on big, tough challenges. I needed to trust that these same ingredients would serve me well in my new adventure. So I took a deep breath and jumped in.

A year and a half later, I can confirm that my instincts were on point. I continue to learn something new almost every day about how best to guide my contribution within the many nuances of the RBC culture, and yet I've found that my core leadership qualities, the ones I had all along, are helping me to succeed.

Looking back, it was certainly a character-building experience to leave Aimia and start over at RBC. But in the end, I learned some incredibly valuable lessons. I learned that no matter how happy you are in a role, or in an organization, you should always stay open to new paths. I also learned how important it is to invest time to build relationships with your networks, both inside and outside your organization. Most importantly, I learned about the power of believing in yourself, as it's that confidence that will always be your greatest strength.

Kim Mason

SENIOR VICE PRESIDENT, BUSINESS DISTRIBUTION,
STRATEGY, AND PERFORMANCE, AT RBC

Pulling Up Roots — to Grow

In 2011 I experienced a major life shift when I was made a senior vice president at RBC and relocated with my family to Halifax from Burlington, Ontario. I'd never lived in Atlantic Canada before, and I didn't know anyone on the RBC team there, or in the community, save for my in-laws. Our kids were 14, 12, and 10 at the time, so adjusting to the change would be challenging for them. And as the first female SVP among all the big banks in the Atlantic region, I knew all eyes would be on me — for sure, I was being sized up! I'd been comfortable in my own environment up until that point, so I also knew that if I was to survive and thrive, I'd have to not only adapt to my new surroundings and do my new job well, but really engage with the community.

So I did my job, but also propelled myself beyond the bank and got out into the community, meeting with its leaders. In time, community members began calling, saying they'd heard I was someone they should meet. I was asked to chair the United Way campaign, and was offered speaking and other community leadership opportunities. Buoyed by the RBC brand and bolstered by the support of its leadership, I enjoyed a feeling of pride in accomplishment — which culminated in 2013 when I was named as one of Canada's Top 25 Women of Influence.

There were roles I'd have never contemplated taking on before, such as when the city's mayor appointed me chair of the Halifax

Stadium Committee. The cause was controversial, as there was much public debate about the merits of Halifax versus Moncton for a stadium; it was Halifax's desire to be a true sports entertainment centre with its own CFL team. Even though I hadn't raised my hand for that job, I transformed my initial reluctance into an opportunity, learning how to be politically astute in a high-profile role and how to deftly manage media coverage while protecting the RBC brand — and my own. It entailed lots of hard work and forged many previously untested skills.

I've often heard that growth comes when we stretch ourselves, and I'm here to tell you that this is so very true. If you want more insights into that, I recommend *The Dip* by Seth Godin; he counsels that you shouldn't just try to survive dips, or setbacks, you should lean into them to truly grow. And as a result of the lessons I've learned, I coach others about reinvention, with a "pay it forward" mentality.

My reinvention isn't over. Since I returned to Toronto in 2014, I've continued to let my curiosity lead me. I engage with colleagues of all ages and backgrounds, and even my own kids, to find out what they're reading, what they're listening to, their hopes and fears. And in the past year I've moved into new strategic roles, one after the other in rapid succession. This means steep learning curves — you're thinking on your feet, you're not necessarily confident in every decision you make, yet you're still expected to lead teams to success. It's humbling. But it also builds your confidence, and it allows your team to see you as vulnerable.

Leadership is a journey that challenges, invigorates, and fulfills. It exhausts, advances, and enlightens. If you get the opportunity to go through this yourself, you'll know how it feels to be at the bottom reach of your internal resources — and how just pushing through can be most liberating.

Pamela Hughes

SENIOR COUNSEL, BLAKE, CASSELS & GRAYDON LLP

Finding a More Flexible Career While Raising Kids

I came up through my career at a time when there weren't many companies with maternity leave policies. In fact, I wrote the mat leave policy for the law firm I worked at when I was pregnant with my second child and wanted to be sure to have some official time off. Seriously.

I didn't take a whole lot of leave — perhaps one month with my first, three months with my second. But when I was at home with my third newborn, I got a phone call from my firm letting me know that I didn't need to come back to work. What can I say? It was simply a different time. I was the only woman securities lawyer at my level, with only one woman being more senior. The systems to support women through the challenges of having a young family weren't there as they are today; there wasn't flex time, nor were there mentoring programs.

Yes, it was hard to accept being asked to leave. But I realized that I'd hung in there too long. Yet I also didn't understand that I needed to be more fully committed to helping my firm grow their business. And I didn't know how to be a better contributor; I have to admit that I went to the office, did my job, then focused on my family.

So now it was time to reinvent my career path and do something that would work for my own life. I decided that government might just be the answer; it had more flexibility than law firms. So I got in touch with Jim Turner at the Ontario Securities Commission. The OSC's chairman, Stan Beck, asked if I was interested in working on negotiating a deal between Canada and the U.S. to create a reciprocity of rules governing public offerings, take-over bids, and continuous disclosure. Without knowing if it was a paid job, I said yes.

Of course it was a paid job. I worked on this project for four years, and it turned out to be the signature achievement of my career. There I was, at age 35, representing Canada in an international negotiation. I was good at it, and developed an expertise in U.S. securities law. That led to me specializing in international securities law for the rest of my career, which I spent at Blakes. I'd turned a career blow into an opportunity to be more successful — and, importantly, an opportunity that was a better fit while I raised three kids.

"Yes, it was hard to accept being asked to leave. But I realized that I'd hung in there too long."

—*Pamela Hughes*

I worked on NAFTA and GATT. In later years, this kind of work often took me away from home for international meetings. My husband was very supportive and helped with the kids while I was away. And the government offered programs that didn't exist in large firms when I was younger. Still, it was challenging work and often left me with feelings of guilt about being away from home.

But one of my most cherished moments was when I was driving our middle son, Andrew, to the airport as he went off to Johns Hopkins University to study medicine. I told him, "I feel bad that

I didn't spend more time focused on you and your brothers when you were young." He replied, "Mom, don't ever worry about that. We didn't know anything different, and we wouldn't be who we are today if you hadn't been so determined and worked so hard. You were our role model."

Heather Fraser

FOUNDER AND CEO, VUKA INNOVATION, INC.

How Do You Manage Risk?

Former colleagues or students of mine often call me for a career chat. The question they always seem to have is this: "How did you do it? How did you find the courage to step off the track and into the unknown?"

Over the years I've been asked that question literally hundreds of times by people who are wrestling with how to switch gears out of their current role or industry. They're conflicted by others' expectations of them, their identity comfort, and the perceived risk of change of any kind.

We often talk about how to manage business risk, but we don't often reflect deeply on professional risk — a very personal decision. People who are looking to "reinvent" think it's risky. I would argue that to not take a calculated risk is the bigger risk.

At five different points in my career I've made a move that others found gutsy, and always at a time when the safest path was to stay put and ascend the known ladder. After 10 years at Procter & Gamble, I had a secure professional path in a company I loved.

I operated a bit outside the norm for the corporate culture, often taking a more creative approach to reframing the business opportunity and collaborating with others to grow the business in new ways. I valued my team and the company's meritocracy. I was clearly "A Corporate Person." But at the height of my career at P&G I wondered, *What if I could be creative all the time?*

At the heart of what I'd been doing was tapping into human insight for inspiration and coming up with innovative ideas that held the promise of human and economic impact. I'd always enjoyed working with agencies, and over the years had courted the idea of moving to the agency side, so I saw that as a natural extension of my passions. It was time to try that path. I made the jump to a great agency: Ogilvy & Mather. Of course, the P&G executives thought I was crazy to leave; my path there had been pretty clear and secure. But I'd earned my stripes, so I figured the worst outcome would be having to go back to the same role in a similar company.

I spent five years at Ogilvy & Mather. It proved to be another good run, with great people making a big impact. Some wonderful mentors and clients helped me become "An Agency Person." I loved the global stage of a first-class agency, but I started to wonder, *What if I could build my own agency with the right partners around a new model for creativity?*

A perfect opportunity came to do just that when I joined the founders of a new agency, TAXI Advertising & Design, as a partner. Again, people wondered how I could step off the known track to what was thought to be a high-risk one. So I asked myself again: What's the worst outcome? Answer: I could go back to the same role or, if the economy went into a tailspin, I could be a brand manager somewhere. So the worst-case scenario was really not so bad — and I became "An Agency Entrepreneur."

Over my 10 years at TAXI I had yet another good ride in the world of ideas, but I missed the world of business. That's when I had a serendipitous opportunity to work with a visionary business-school dean at the University of Toronto and bring the worlds of business and creativity together in a new initiative that could reinvent business education. I'd always been dedicated to unleashing others' potential, so it seemed like a natural move. On a more personal level, my parents had become quite ill, and I was their guardian. When one died (shortly before the next) and I was completely heartbroken, I had a moment of realization: We're *all* going to die (duh), so you might as well do something meaningful with your life. I duly became "A Pracademic" — a person who connects learning and practice and bridges creativity and business.

My answer to the "What's the worst-case scenario?" question got more extreme: If this doesn't work, I could always be some sort of innovation consultant — I had the credentials for that. And if I couldn't get any projects on my own, I could always be a waitress. I'd get to chat with people all day, then go home and not worry about work. That didn't sound so bad to me.

That pracademic move set me on a totally new and exciting trajectory. I got to work with some of the smartest people in their fields, a lot of blue-chip organizations around the world, and a stream of bright, ambitious graduate students. Then I wrote a book, called *Design Works*. Now I was "An Author."

But I had one more shift I wanted to try, one that would combine all my passions with an ambition to help more people realize their potential to innovate, to turn ideas into business.

So I started up a small practice outside the academic realm called Vuka Innovation. With a keen group of graduates, we extended the principles of my book into a deeper dive into the discipline I helped define as "business design," helping organizations boost their capacity to innovate through knowledge and skill transfer. The ultimate vision was to scale that know-how into a software play. Now I'd transitioned from a consulting service into "A Tech Start-Up."

I saw all these reinventions as a natural evolution based on my core purpose, values, and passions. Taking a so-called risk is about asking yourself whether the potential regret of *not* following your intuition and dreams is greater than the risk of the worst-case scenario. It's a personal decision. But I would argue that worst case is probably not that bad. And being true to your aspirations will keep you happier, and younger, for a long time.

Shari Walczak

CO-FOUNDER AND CHIEF STRATEGY OFFICER, THE GARDEN NORTH AMERICA INC.

Stepping Out of a Big Job to Launch a New Venture

Back in the mid-1990s, I was working for one of Canada's top-tier advertising agencies. My boss and I had been successfully shaping a niche business within the agency when suddenly everything changed: he announced he would be leaving to accept the opportunity of a lifetime.

The executive team felt they needed to find a heavy-hitter replacement from outside. Sensing an opportunity — and ignoring that inside voice that told me I was "too young," "not senior enough," "lacking in credibility" — I set about preparing a business plan that would allow me to continue building what we'd started together. After presenting to the president and senior VPs, I created an "easy yes" situation for them: Give me the chance to implement this plan over the next six months and, if successful, let me take over this new division. And if I couldn't deliver the desired results, I would happily return to the more traditional career path I'd already been pursuing in account management.

I landed the job. Had I waited, a replacement would have likely been found, and I would have continued as the person helping to deliver someone else's vision. This move reinvented the trajectory of my career and gave me my first taste of leadership.

> **"I try never to allow a fear of failure to hold me back from trying something new, or from following an ambition that others question."**
>
> —*Shari Walczak*

I try never to allow a fear of failure to hold me back from trying something new, or from following an ambition that others question. Several years ago, I reinvented my career again. And yet at first I was plagued with self-doubt. I was in talks to leave the corporate agency world to establish an independent venture, but as the business idea began to take shape and we were close to transforming talk into reality, I started to question the wisdom of following this path: Would I be jeopardizing the financial stability of my family? How would we continue saving for our children's education? If this venture were to fail, would my career in this industry be over?

I had frank, honest conversations with my business partner and my life partner, both of whom not only reaffirmed their faith in my ability to do this but also made it crystal clear that pursuing an entrepreneurial venture wasn't a career-ending move; it wouldn't wipe out the two decades of experience I'd already accumulated. My support network transformed my self-doubt and gave me the confidence to submit my resignation, step out of my comfort zone, and launch The Garden North America Inc., the creative and brand strategy agency I co-own.

I've learned that opportunity, ambition, and success look very different for every individual and often come in an unexpected wrapping. So if you limit yourself to a traditional definition of success or rigidly stick to the "establishment" career path, you may overlook your true calling.

GOOD ADVICE
The PPCO Approach

Even now, with more than 20 years of professional experience, I can't say I've completely overcome self-doubt and the inevitable "imposter syndrome." But whenever they creep into my personal narrative, I drown out the negative inside voice by (1) revisiting the proof points from my past successes and (2) developing an inspiring vision of what might come to fruition if I just go for it.

A tool I use to overcome fear is something I was introduced to while doing my master's degree in Creativity & Change Leadership. PPCO is a four-stage process for thinking through an idea, opportunity, or initiative. I consider these:

Positives. I list all the positive facets of the idea under consideration — what do I like about it?

Potentials. I describe all the potential outcomes that might result from the pursuit or implementation of this idea.

Concerns. Rather than generating a long list of cons, I reframe my potential concerns as questions, or problems to be solved. For example, instead of listing "reduced salary," I'd write it as "How might I replace the income that will be lost while pursuing this opportunity?" or "What are all the ways we can reduce household costs to make up for the reduction of income?"

Overcoming concerns. Armed with my list of concerns, I tackle them one by one, moving from most concerning to least concerning by conducting a rapid-fire ideation. I often include my spouse and/or a close friend or two. This generates at least five potential ideas for how to overcome each concern.

Inevitably, the PPCO approach helps me to methodically think through a situation and then decide on a course of action I can feel confident about.

—Shari Walczak

"**My mother had this wisdom that kids are small for just a short time and that life gets easier after five or six years, when they start school.**"

—Beatrix Dart

Beatrix Dart

FOUNDER AND EXECUTIVE DIRECTOR, ROTMAN INITIATIVE
FOR WOMEN IN BUSINESS; PROFESSOR OF STRATEGIC MANAGEMENT

From Consulting Back to Academia

I've always been quite ambitious, and have thrived on being a high achiever. I went for a Ph.D. in statistics and economics because it was challenging and I wanted to reach for the top. When I applied for a management consulting role at a leading consulting firm I had only a vague notion of what that might mean on a day-to-day basis, but again, I loved the idea of being challenged and working for a highly regarded organization that came with lots of international travel.

Family planning was a concept I took for granted — having children is after all the natural progression for women, right? Up until then I viewed my workplace as having no gender obstacles, that advancing was completely merit-based — do well, move up. But six years into my job at that consulting firm I had a child, and after I returned from four months of maternity leave it became clear that the decision to enter motherhood truly does change your career path. I found myself contemplating how my career would need to take a backseat to family demands. In hindsight, I think I gave in to an expectation from my family, from my peers, and from societal stereotypes that making my children my first priority was the right way forward.

All of this added up to pressure on me to find a job or profession that would allow for more flexibility. I wasn't prepared to become a stay-at-home mom; I simply had too much invested in my education and career to imagine feeling fulfilled by being a caregiver and housekeeper.

So I reinvented my career and went back to the world of academia — something that felt like a much better fit, thanks to the strong female role models I'd had growing up in Switzerland who always emphasized the importance of education.

My grandmother was from Poland, and had survived 12 years in a Russian prison camp during World War II. At the time, my mother was a young girl and had to spend those 12 years in an orphanage. When my grandmother got out of the prison camp and finally found her three children again, they emigrated to Switzerland. They had to create a life as war refugees in a new country.

My mother was very bright but never had the chance to go to university, though she was always a working mom. She worked in a chemical laboratory. When I was growing up, my grandmother and mother both encouraged me to go to university. They instilled in me that material things aren't really important because they can be taken away from you or disappear at any time. What is truly important, they said, is education; that's something nobody can ever take away. This created my value system. These amazing women were survivors; they were very focused on making the best of their lives.

Because of this, I always considered it a privilege to have the opportunity to go to school and receive the gift of education. That feeling has never gone away. I believe that an education is something you have to nourish and grow to make the most out of it — just as I believe that if you have a privileged position in life, you should use it to make society better and help others.

When I was deciding to make the transition back to academia, my mother was fiercely on my side. We'd talk on the phone, and although I knew it was possible to have a career *and* children, she always reinforced that perspective. She had this wisdom that kids are small for just a short time and that life gets easier after five or six years, when they start school. Her outlook matched mine: "Don't give up your career just to make it easier right now."

I feel lucky that I was able to join Rotman as professor and academic director in 2000. It was a great fit because I could apply my knowledge of the business world to business education. The dean, Roger Martin, hired me to look at ways to improve the executive degree programs, and I wasn't shy about going to the market and asking how to design programs to better suit the needs of the market. Based on that feedback, we ended up designing the first one-year EMBA program in Canada. And in 2007, I had the opportunity to participate in The Judy Project. It was a fascinating experience. Everybody was blown away by the power of that week together, collecting insights and reflecting on them with others. It was the most valuable educational experience I've ever had. (For more on the program, see the "Staying In" chapter on page 203.)

The bottom line is that a career in education is a very happy place for me. It's a dream come true to have the chance to help others and advance people in their careers. I wake up every morning feeling inspired and motivated.

I mentor quite a few younger women and also interact with business people from a wide variety of backgrounds. I encourage all of them to challenge the assumptions, beliefs, and stereotypes that society puts forward. We run a program to support women who want to return to work after an often lengthy leave of absence. Many of them have deep regrets that they allowed their careers to collapse, and will admit that they put on a brave face because they felt society expected it from them.

I say, if you feel comfortable and excited by being a stay-at-home mom, then that's great. But if you're always taking a back-seat and your ambitions aren't allowed, then speak up. It's surprising

to me how few women have had a conversation with their partners about what they want out of life. It's a wake-up call for your
partner, too, to have that conversation and for you to be able to
communicate that you want to use your brain for things other than
supporting family life.

Women need to be honest with themselves: What makes you
fulfilled? Everyone has different dreams, and yours may or may not
be to make it to the CEO's office. The important thing is to take the
first steps: reflecting on and then communicating your ambition.

9

Generosity

When you contribute to a non-profit cause in Canada or elsewhere, you show your generosity as a global citizen. But generosity is an important leadership characteristic in the corporate context, too.

You can demonstrate generosity when you allow other people on your team to take credit for their work, or when you thank them for their contribution. It's reflected in the way people view you as a leader. If you hog the puck and don't allow others to take credit for their work, your team will see that right away. They'll view you as a control freak, insecure. If, on the other hand, you're generous, it will show that you're confident enough to let other people share in the glory.

When you agree to sponsor or mentor, for instance, you're paying it forward in one of the strongest demonstrations of corporate generosity. I often ask women and men in my network to take a meeting, offer their advice on a young entrepreneur's business plan, and otherwise provide them with guidance or support. This is my absolute favourite form of generosity. We're simply paying back someone who guided us along the way! And by doing so we're building tomorrow's companies, community, and economy with talent. A payback that is immeasurable.

Shelly Lazarus

CHAIRMAN EMERITUS, OGILVY & MATHER

Sharing the Problem

One of the inherent qualities of true leaders that nobody talks about is generosity. It's critical in leading other people. Great leaders share the problem, and they share the opportunities. They come together and work in teams to figure out how to solve something. People who lead do so with others; they share everything with them — including, very importantly, the credit at the end. And it's a virtuous circle, since the next time an opportunity arises, those same people will want to sign up with you again.

If you want the best team, your compassion or empathy, your generosity, is something others will be attracted to immediately. They can feel it. And these kinds of leaders get the superstars to want to be on their team.

> "If you want the best team, your compassion or empathy, your generosity, is something others will be attracted to immediately."
>
> —*Shelly Lazarus*

The best speech I've ever heard on team building was all about sharing the problem, a hallmark of a generous leader. It was given by an ethnographer at Cambridge University who'd spent months studying the Cambridge rowing team — from the season's first tryouts to the final race against Oxford, their arch rival. (It was a race Cambridge had lost the seven previous years.)

He was interested in how teams got built, and noted that the A-team wasn't made up of the eight fastest rowers. Technical competence was traded off for social intelligence: the rowers selected were those deemed best at pulling the crew together as a unit. Cambridge won the race.

The idea that you as leader have the best ideas and are the smartest person in the room is not a winning proposition. You have to build a team, a great team … and trust them to get on with it.

Shale Hajiyeva

EXECUTIVE DIRECTOR, AZERBAIJAN MICRO-FINANCE ASSOCIATION

It Takes a Village

I never take for granted the comfort of my office on the fifth floor of the Caspian Plaza building in central Baku, the capital of Azerbaijan. That's because much of the time I'm out travelling in the mountainous regions of my home country, which is sandwiched between Iran to the south and Russia to the north. The Caspian Sea lies to the east. I've become accustomed to staying in very basic hotels that aren't heated in winter and are too hot in the summer.

But the people I regularly visit as part of my work have to live in uncomfortable conditions each day, and the positive impact our projects have on them more than compensates for any of my own discomfort. To date, we've implemented more than 50 projects for rural women from low-income families. These people have been encouraged to become entrepreneurs in order to support their families. That makes me very happy.

What is micro-finance? It's financial services — loans, savings, insurance, and fund transfers — for entrepreneurs, small businesses, and individuals who lack access to traditional banking services. The Azerbaijan Micro-Finance Association (AMFA) supports its member organizations that provide the loans, and we give training and support for business plan preparation. We also offer seed capital for start-ups and are hoping to develop a mentorship program for rural women in business.

I've been fortunate enough to do well in this role thanks to mentorship from Jennifer Lee, a Canadian woman I met in 2006 when she was invited here to help develop the financial sector in Azerbaijan, which gained independence from the Soviet Union in 1991. (At the time she was with Bell Canada, but is now a partner at Deloitte.) I learned a lot from Jennifer, and will always be grateful for her guidance — and for recommending me for a scholarship with The Judy Project, which I attended in 2008.

> "WHEN I SEE REAL IMPROVEMENTS TO THE
> LIVELIHOODS OF WOMEN WHO COULD ONLY
> HAVE DREAMED OF HAVING HOT WATER IN
> THEIR BATHROOM AND KITCHEN, OR HAVING
> A SOFA TO SIT ON RATHER THAN THE FLOOR,
> IT'S VERY MOTIVATING."
>
> *—Jhale Hajiyeva*

Jennifer's mentorship, and The Judy Project, completely transformed me and therefore the AMFA as an institution. I gained inner strength as a leader, and became crystal clear on what we had to accomplish. It enabled me to help develop our first three-year strategic plan and a detailed business plan. The execution of these plans marked the start of what has become a success story for the

AMFA and for my own growth, both personally and professionally. We got our first international award, Micro-Finance Network of the Year, in 2017. Through it all, my husband has been wonderfully encouraging and supportive, helping care for our daughter whenever I'm away at international meetings — and never complaining if dinner is late!

The AMFA has helped borrowers across Azerbaijan — 98 percent of them women. One, for instance, attended our business-plan training, and ended up starting a home business: her mother-in-law convinced her to put to use her excellent skills in preparing homemade spaghetti, along with a flatbread called *lavash* and the traditional Azerbaijani dishes *gutab* and *kete* (flat pies with meat or vegetables) to sell in her village. Her products became so popular in the surrounding villages that she introduced a delivery service — via her husband on his motorcycle. She recently borrowed US$250 from her local micro-finance institution to expand her business.

Another woman started a home-based business in her village, baking cakes for special occasions like birthday parties, engagement ceremonies, and anniversary celebrations. She took out a loan of US$300 from a micro-finance institution to do so. We learned recently that she'd become sick, and was no longer able to work. She was going to have to shut down her business, but then her 18-year-old daughter stepped in; the girl was confident that she'd learned enough from her mother about baking the cakes. We were very happy to hear that the daughter is getting enough orders to cover her mother's medical treatments *and* keep up with the loan repayments.

When I see real improvements to the livelihoods of women who could only have dreamed of having hot water in their bathroom and kitchen, or having a sofa to sit on rather than the floor, it's very motivating. I realize that we can't bring change to each rural woman's life, but at least we can do our piece to reduce the number of those who lack access to basic comforts. Every woman who passes our training gets a rare chance to be equipped with the necessary tools and guidance to change not only her own life but the lives of others in her community.

And for me personally, thanks to all the support I've received over the years to grow myself as a leader, I've gained self-confidence. I feel strongly that whatever you dream of achieving in your life is possible if you believe in yourself.

Pamela Hughes

SENIOR COUNSEL, BLAKE, CASSELS & GRAYDON LLP

How Working Pro Bono Led to the Zomba Prison Project

In the spring of 2017 I found myself sitting in a plastic chair tapping my foot to the sounds of the Zomba Prison Project, a band of musicians made up of prisoners and staff at Zomba maximum security prison, some 300 kilometres south of the capital of Malawi in southern Africa.

I was there to see this Grammy-nominated band as part of my role on the board of Dignitas International, a Canadian charity that does health work in Malawi. Dignitas had implemented a health care program in this notoriously overcrowded prison with terrible conditions, and now the band was treating us to a show to thank the organization.

This was my second time in Malawi for Dignitas, one of three charitable boards I work on. I'd felt that after a fulfilling career as a securities lawyer it was time to do some pro bono work. In my capacity as vice chair I've helped train the African lawyers and judges writing Malawi's new constitution, and have worked with passionate, intelligent, committed people I would not otherwise have had an opportunity to meet.

> "**I WANTED TO GET INVOLVED WITH CHARITABLE BOARDS BECAUSE I KNOW THAT WORK CAN BECOME SO FOCUSED ON MONEY.**"
>
> —*Pamela Hughes*

I wanted to get involved with these boards because I know that work can become so focused on money, especially when you work in law firms and alongside investment banks, and it was important to me to pursue fulfillment in another aspect of my life. It was a transition that began when my last child went to university and I needed something to fill the emotional gap. I was also able to bring in Blakes to do pro bono work with these organizations.

It was very special to be a part of this unforgettable experience, and as I listened to that beautiful music and breathed in the warm evening air, I reflected on the fact that throughout your career you can contribute in so many meaningful ways.

THE MOMENT

As I listened to that beautiful music and breathed in the warm evening air, I reflected on the fact that throughout your career you can contribute in so many meaningful ways.

Charlotte Beers

FORMER CHAIR AND CEO, OGILVY & MATHER

Generosity of Spirit

Oddly enough, being known for a certain kind of generosity is one of the secret ingredients of being seen as a leader. When that tight little management group or board is trying to decide who to promote to the big job, they know they're taking a leap of faith. So they focus on a few things. One is breadth of talent, something you're working every day to demonstrate. Another is an indefinable something called presence — that wonderful aura that surrounds you the more you learn to speak up and show what you're made of.

> "WHAT IF I'D MISSED THAT CHANCE TO BE GENEROUS, SWIMMING IN MY OWN UNCERTAINTY AND INFLUENCED BY THE COMMONLY HELD AND LIMITED DEFINITION OF WHAT IT MEANS TO BE STRONG AND TOUGH?"
>
> —*Charlotte Beers*

And then there's generosity of spirit. It's interesting: the higher we go, the more we're in danger of losing our sense of generosity to others. The air gets thinner, and there are more unwritten rules of behaviour — and far more complex relationships. In these elite echelons, it's tempting to get tougher, more demanding, and impatient with people who might slow our momentum.

But at times of intense pressure when you need to compete more fiercely, you should step back and call up your generosity of spirit. Call up respect, that first cousin of generosity. Every single person you work with deserves your respect.

I teach an executive woman's class, and one attendee said recently, "I don't suffer fools lightly." But such a sentiment really means "Only the best will do — someone as good as I am." Great leaders are known for their treasure-hunting skills ... finding that special something in the "fools" and embracing them so that they're lifted up, their performance magnified. That's generosity.

I learned a lot about this potent ingredient of leadership in the weeks before I was to take the chairman and CEO job at Ogilvy & Mather, a worldwide advertising agency of some 8000 people and 300 offices. I was replacing a CEO who'd been the second or third in that position in recent times, as the company was faltering badly. People had been let go, and many of the agency's stars were leaving as fast as the clients were.

WPP had recently acquired Ogilvy, and had spent some months talking to me privately about taking the job of CEO. This was sure to be a controversial move, as I was coming from a medium-sized agency with little international experience — and, oh yes, I was a girl. The first one. A glass-ceiling breaker.

Standing in the shards, living in a hotel, I knew not one Ogilvy client nor any key Ogilvy people. No one knew I was coming in except the CEO I was replacing. He invited me to dinner, and it was clear he was tired and discouraged. I liked him. Then I surprised him by asking him to draft a version of how he'd like to introduce me to the people of Ogilvy. The expectation had been that WPP would be the ones to announce my new role with some fanfare while giving a rather abrupt farewell to the outgoing CEO. But I didn't want this good man to be diminished.

So he introduced me as his choice, and got to tell his story about why he was leaving. I just didn't feel any need to brandish the victory sword. We all had a lot to do and much to prove.

But the big guys down the hall thought I went way too far in my next move: I offered the dethroned CEO a chance to stay for a while and work on the key Ford account.

My fellow managers felt this weakened my hold on the CEO title, warning that it would be dangerous to keep a dissident aboard. I felt no threat; I was aware that I had an ocean of things to learn, and this fine man was teaching me every day. One of the components of being brave enough to be generous is your willingness to challenge common wisdom. I respected this man, and in doing so he returned the gift by guiding me. Months later, the time was right to part ways.

But for me, the best part of that experience happened 11 years later at a company event. The wife of my preceding CEO approached me shyly and said, "I'll never forget what you did for my husband. It made such a difference to us."

I left the event with tears in my eyes. What if I'd missed that chance to be generous, swimming in my own uncertainty and influenced by the commonly held and limited definition of what it means to be strong and tough?

Yes, show them who's in charge. But be generous when it's not easy or obvious, even when it's risky and uncomfortable. Bravery, self-esteem, and respect: that's the brew from which generosity comes in the workplace.

10
Authenticity

The best leaders are authentic. They're the same human being whether they're at the office, in the community, or at home. When they speak their voice is clear and true, and as the listener, you know it's coming from a real place. Authenticity is also conveyed through actions and behaviours. We all know what bad acting looks like on stage and in the boardroom.

The sycophantic VP in Marketing will be found out and won't progress — maybe not this week, but eventually. The lack of authenticity is a fatal flaw. In an increasingly transparent world — where the borders between life and work are being erased and social media is stalking your identity — it's just too hard to maintain a persona different from who you really are.

When a leader is authentic, she's understandable and real. Her commitment and passion are visible. She is someone you want to follow.

Andrea Stairs

GENERAL MANAGER, EBAY CANADA
& LATIN AMERICA

Becoming a Better Leader

When you're first promoted to a leadership position, nobody teaches you how to be a great leader; and, in some cases, you need to ask for help, which takes courage. The insights I received at The Judy Project helped me become a better leader. How?

Showing your vulnerability. When I started out leading eBay Canada, my first inclination was to lead from the front, to be the general in control and to avoid showing vulnerability. I thought that by projecting strength and confidence I would inspire trust and security in my new team. But our employment satisfaction surveys showed I was going in the wrong direction. I got feedback that people weren't feeling confident, and that the way I was leading was eroding trust and distancing me from the team.

What to do? I put my pride aside and owned my mistake. I told everyone that I recognized the need to adjust my leadership style and that from now on I'd be different — more transparent. I also committed to investing in becoming a better leader. Among other things, I got a personal coach. Now I take the time to connect authentically with my team; I tell them what's happening in the business and how I'm feeling about it. You have to have the courage as a leader to share measured vulnerability — the trust and confidence you'll build with your team is well worth it.

Being a role model for your children. One thing that has never been a leap of faith for me is my attitude toward being a working mom. I have two kids, a seven-year-old boy and a four-year-old girl. I've always felt lucky to have a living role model in my own mother for how to have a family and a fulfilling career. As a girl, I felt involved in her career — I knew what was going on and I understood the importance of what she was doing (and the pleasure and satisfaction she got from it).

While many working women struggle with feelings of guilt, I hold a deep belief that my career directly benefits my kids. The fact that both my husband and I work allows us to provide for our family, but I'm convinced that our dedication to our careers is also arming our kids with what they'll need to be successful in their later life. Daily, our kids have tangible demonstrations that we love our work and are rewarded by it — my hope is that our examples help to ensure they find the same things in their future. That's not to say that I don't have to make tough choices, but I know I'm giving my kids a healthy sense of reality that includes balance and inspiration.

I recently came home and told my kids I'd received a leadership award from the Women's Executive Network, and they were excited. "What did you get it for?" my son asked. "I'm a leader," I told him. His eyes went wide. My kids can see that I'm legitimately proud of my accomplishments, and they're proud of me, too.

> "HAVING AN AUTHENTIC CONVERSATION WITH YOUR BOSS BEFORE YOU GO ON MATERNITY LEAVE CAN BE YOUR WAY OF CONTROLLING THE NARRATIVE."
>
> —*Tina Lee*

Tina Lee

CEO, T&T SUPERMARKETS

Being Authentic as Moms-to-Be

I have a five-year-old, a three-year-old, and I'm pregnant with my third. If you're in baby-making mode like me, here's one tip: Be authentic with your boss, and have a heart-to-heart conversation with them about your maternity leave plans. As awkward as it may be, especially with a male boss, try to open up and share — and know that this isn't just a personal discussion, it's a professional discussion. Share things like how long you plan to be on leave, if and how much you want to stay connected while you're at home, and what your own expectations are of your job when you return.

Many women shy away from this conversation because they think it's going be held against them somehow, especially if the manager is a man. But let's give the guys some credit — most men in our professional lives are also fathers, brothers, and husbands, and totally get what women go through in bringing life into this world. You may be surprised how having the conversation in the first place ends up putting you at ease about work before you take time off. It will help build a trusting relationship with your boss, give you more control over your career, and help the company plan for your return in a meaningful way that matches your expectations.

Women face enough headwinds making progress in the corporate world: a shrinking pipeline to leadership positions, the gender wage gap, and unconscious gender biases. The biggest attrition of women in the workforce is during the child-bearing years. Having this authentic conversation with your boss before you go on maternity leave can be your way of controlling the narrative, and it will show you care about your career. Avoiding the conversation might just leave your career to the whims of gender biases.

Shelly Lazarus

CHAIRMAN EMERITUS, OGILVY & MATHER

Eat in the Cafeteria from Time to Time

Leadership brings power. That is the nature of it. But with power can come isolation, a separation from the very people and activities that got you to the position in the first place. The newspapers are littered with stories of leaders who fell from grace for seemingly stupid mistakes.

In his book *Collapse*, UCLA professor Jared Diamond cites leaders' isolation from their people as the dominant reason for the collapse of civilizations. The leaders are so cut off that they don't understand the plight of the people (the Marie Antoinette syndrome) … and therefore do nothing until it's too late.

My advice: Eat in the cafeteria from time to time. Talk to people in the elevator. Invite people three layers down from you to have coffee in your office. This isn't brain science. It just makes sense to keep engaged, to listen and learn. For you to be a strong leader you have to have that connection. So one day, when you wield power, don't let it go to your head. Stay humble.

Sandy Sharman

SENIOR EXECUTIVE VICE PRESIDENT AND
CHIEF HUMAN RESOURCES AND
COMMUNICATIONS OFFICER, CIBC

A Heart to Heart with Myself

The year I turned 35 was a particularly demanding time. I loved my job, I loved my family; life was good. But I was running at the speed of light and questioning the purpose of it all. So I decided to sit down and have a heart-to-heart talk with myself about what I really wanted. And then I wrote myself three promises. These promises would create the foundation for my choices going forward, and ensure that I'd stay true to my authentic self. They'd help ensure that I wouldn't change for the sake of work at the expense of everything else that was dear to me. And they would help me to be successful. I committed to staying real by …

Always being there for my children's milestones. I knew I might be the last parent to run in and grab a seat at a school play, but I would be there.

Ensuring that our financial future and retirement was secure. To be fully transparent, what I actually wrote down was, "Don't screw up the finances!"

Achieving these goals as a family team. At the end of the day, I wanted to be able to look my husband and kids in the eyes, and for all of us to know that we did it together.

"I WROTE MYSELF THREE PROMISES. THESE PROMISES WOULD CREATE THE FOUNDATION FOR MY CHOICES GOING FORWARD, AND ENSURE THAT I'D STAY TRUE TO MY AUTHENTIC SELF."

—*Sandy Sharman*

Fast-forward a few years. When I was recently promoted to my current role, my husband and two sons and I celebrated at our special place in cottage country. Together, the four of us popped the champagne bottle and gave a toast to "us." I even delivered a little speech: "This isn't *my* new job. It's *our* new job. We achieved this together." We talked about how we'd each contributed to our collective success as a family by staying the course. And we were more aware than ever before how wonderful life is when you keep it real and accomplish your dreams together.

Lorna Borenstein

FOUNDER AND CEO, GROKKER

Never Be Embarrassed to Be You

Early in my career at Hewlett Packard there was a big company event, and the CEO, Lewis Platt, spoke. Afterward, everyone — there were hundreds of us — lined up for a meet and greet with him. Each person shook his hand in turn as my boss and I got closer to the front. She was an amazing senior executive whom I really admired, in part for being so warm and genuine.

When we reached Lew, instead of shaking his hand, my boss pulled him in for a hug. "So nice to see you!" she said, and then gave him a peck on the cheek! I was scandalized, thinking it undermined her credibility as an executive, because this was *not* what the sea of navy-suited, handshaking men were doing.

When I asked her about it judgmentally afterward, she taught me an invaluable lesson. "How many hands did he shake tonight?" she asked me. It was literally hundreds. "And how many hugs did he get?" She paused to let this sink in, then said, "That was genuine. When I greet people I care about, I hug them. Never forget that you're a woman; never be embarrassed to be you." In that moment, my boss taught me how to just be myself.

THE MOMENT

"Never forget that you're a woman; never be embarrassed to be you." In that moment, my boss taught me how to just be myself.

To this day, whenever I finish a business meeting — assuming it went well and I feel a good connection with the others — as everyone is leaving, I say, "I'm a hugger," and I do just that. Ninety percent of the time, they reciprocate. My boss was right. When you hug someone and it's genuine, that really does break through at a level that's surprising and wonderful.

It's true that in this current atmosphere of tensions between men and women in the workplace, men often don't know how they should interact with women. When the topic comes up and a man whom I *know* isn't a harasser says "I don't know how to be friendly anymore," I joke, "Just don't grab her ass and you'll be fine." What

I'm trying to say to them is that if they're respectful and authentic, they don't have to worry; they're not doing anything wrong.

GOOD ADVICE
How to Deal with Mother's Guilt

There's a piece of advice I want to share about how to deal with all the guilt that comes with being a career mom. Believe me, my daughter Megan can tell you some "bad mother" stories. (Here's one: Once, when she was a schoolgirl and said she felt sick, my response was to send her to school with two little Tylenols in her pocket, telling her, "If you start feeling a bit hot, just take one of these." Turns out she had scarlet fever.)

I felt bad about not being there for Megan as much as I would have liked to when she was young. Yet she (and her friends) have always been very proud of me as a working mom, and she's tougher for having had the upbringing that she did. I want to drive home the message that you can prioritize your career and still raise well-adjusted kids.

I would love for my daughter, who is now a lawyer, to share with my colleagues how much she admired me when she was growing up, and how much she still does! I want to tell all the mothers who are feeling torn for pursuing their career goals that being an effective female role model requires this high level of commitment. Trust me: the kids will turn out fine.

—**Jane Kinney**
Vice Chair, Deloitte LLP

Cathy Barrick

CEO, ALZHEIMER SOCIETY OF ONTARIO

"Go Get 'Em, Tiger!"

One morning at work, back when I was in my early twenties, I received flowers from my then husband. They were tiger lilies, and the card read, "Go get 'em, tiger!"

That was the day I was going to confront my boss. He was domineering, outspoken, and mean. He intimidated me — and I let him. It was completely out of character for me to be meek; if you knew me, you'd agree that back then I was every bit as outgoing and true to myself as I am now. But working for that boss, I felt I couldn't express myself fully. Part of it was being young and less confident in my abilities — especially when I was challenged by my boss. But still, I knew that how he was treating me wasn't right. So I decided to take matters into my own hands.

I asked to meet with him to have a discussion. Shaking in my seat, I told him that his behaviour was intimidating and interfered with our ability to work together. I asked him to think about how he spoke to me in the future.

The conversation went … okay. My boss was somewhat open to listening — not his strong suit. And in our meeting he did soften a bit, and told me that he appreciated my saying something. He even gave me a bit of a pep talk about how it's okay to disagree with people sometimes. I think it was lip service, because afterward his behaviour didn't change much.

But what did change was *me*. That was my first lesson in how to stand up for myself and be true to the authentic me. I've used those skills many times since, not only in challenging others if needed, but in presenting myself in a way that doesn't give much room for intimidation. That confrontation gave me the know-how to face these situations head on throughout my career.

People who work with me today will describe me as real. I have fun at work. I laugh with coworkers, and sometimes cry if the situation calls for it. I make an effort to get to know staff personally. I meet with all new staff when they start and with all other staff throughout the year. You'll see me wandering the halls regularly, stopping by to say hello. I harness my strengths.

Do *you*. Be authentic, and grab hold of all your strengths — and weaknesses — and bring them with you full force everywhere you go.

LETTER TO MY DAUGHTER

Kerri-Ann Santaguida
Vice President and General Manager, Merchant
Services, American Express Canada

Dear Laura,

Though you're only 13, you're not too young for me to share with you this piece of advice about your future: Make sure you choose a career that revolves around something you enjoy and are passionate about. Life is too precious to spend time in a role or organization that doesn't bring you happiness or fuel your personal dreams.

Once you're there, surround yourself with mentors and sponsors for support — but trust your own instincts. It's so important to stay true to yourself and to your values. Remember, too, that change is another word for opportunity; embrace it as a chance to grow, to learn, and to chart your course to an unknown path.

Most importantly, never stop managing your career with intent. I always say that I'm a mother first and an executive second, and as such I've had to play a very active role in managing my career rather than simply letting it happen to me. I planned, and made strategic decisions. I gathered the confidence to articulate my values and needs. I was fluid when I needed to be, but always stayed firm to my dreams.

When you hold yourself to a standard and show others what you can do, they will start to embrace and respect your values. My leadership, performance, and proven ability to deliver on results and communicate my values to my leaders and the organization are what allowed those around me to embrace and respect my views and priorities. No one else is going to do that for you, Laura, so it's key that you be an active participant in your own career path. This is your journey: Be the CEO of *you*.

Love,
Mom

"**A** CONFRONTATION WITH MY BOSS AS A YOUNG WOMAN GAVE ME THE KNOW-HOW TO FACE THESE SITUATIONS HEAD ON THROUGHOUT MY CAREER."

—*Cathy Barrick*

Sarah Davis

PRESIDENT, LOBLAW COMPANIES LIMITED

How Authenticity Can Lead to Success

Standing on the stage at the Loblaw AGM in May 2017, in the former Maple Leaf Gardens in downtown Toronto, I thought, *I guess you can be nice and still have success.*

Back when I told my parents that I wanted to go the corporate route, they warned me that I was never going to make it in the tough world of business; even my grandmother had said I was "too nice for this life." But here I was, about to make a presentation to shareholders and board members. And Galen Weston, our chairman and CEO, had for the first time as far as I could remember (I'd been there for 10 years and had just been promoted) invited his president to join him on stage.

After I gave the presentation, we took questions. One young woman asked me if I had any advice on how to be successful. I gave the following reply:

1. Work hard.

2. Be the person people can always count on. When you're given something to do, get it done and do it well.

3. Don't let being a woman be an excuse for not achieving something. Because if you do, you become a victim.

4. Be kind. The world can use more kindness. Kindness doesn't make you weak. You can be kind in business and still be a good leader.

It was the fourth point about being kind that surprised some people. But that's the authentic me, and I think authenticity plays a key role in success.

My parents didn't think the corporate world would be the right fit for my personality. My mother was a teacher and my father was a professor; nobody in our family had gone into business. Even though I was very good at math, they thought I should get a job that focused on softer skills. Despite their advice, I went to business school and decided to prove to the world that you can be in business and still be a kind person.

"YOU DON'T NEED TO BE A MAN TO BE SUCCESSFUL. AND YOU DON'T NEED TO BE AGGRESSIVE TO BE SUCCESSFUL. YOU NEED TO BE YOURSELF."
—*Sarah Davis*

In my first job at Rogers I was an analyst, and my boss's boss's boss was the CFO. He saw something in me, and would invite me into management meetings full of senior people in their forties and fifties. I was insecure in that setting, as you can imagine, yet he made me feel I belonged. At first he allowed me to present topics that weren't controversial in order to get me feeling comfortable about being there. Each time I went it became easier to discuss more difficult subjects. He staged my success, and that was super kind of him. He eventually made me feel comfortable, like I belonged in a place where I really didn't.

It only inspired me to remain true to myself and my innate character traits. I had the chance to pay the kindness forward when I joined Bell. I was in finance, and had been doing all the board reporting. A younger man, probably in his late twenties, joined as the CFO, and part of his job was to present to the board — in a boardroom full of older people who might not go easy on you if you weren't fully prepared. Even though I worked for him, I felt I could give him some advice. I helped him prepare for those meetings, and told him what to expect. He'd come back and thank me, saying it had worked really well. I felt so vested in his success. His first call after the big meetings was always to me, letting me know how it had gone — he knew I actually cared. I learned to do the same for others over the years, because when he thanked me it felt great, and I wanted to share that feeling of being part of something.

Don't get me wrong. I can be tough. I do call people out when I need to and I do make hard decisions, but never out of maliciousness. It always comes from a need to make our business more successful.

You don't need to be a man to be successful. And you don't need to be aggressive to be successful. You need to be yourself. If that means being honest and kind, then the world will be a better place.

Lindsay Sacknoff

SENIOR VICE PRESIDENT, HEAD OF U.S CONTACT CENTRES, TD BANK

The Value of Getting in the Trenches

"So, Lindsay," my mom asked again. "What are you going to do for a living?"

"I don't know … drive a Zamboni?" I was only half joking — I was a big Boston Bruins fan, after all, and used to play hockey in high school. Now I was in my last year at Vanderbilt University in Nashville, where I'd majored in economics and psychology. My parents and friends had taken to asking me what I wanted to do with my life, and it drove them nuts that I just didn't know yet. But I'd never been the type to take a set path toward a predetermined goal. I liked to enjoy the journey.

That fact — that I want to like the people I worked with and be inspired by what I was doing — accidentally became clear soon after, and set the course of my career. A close girlfriend of mine wanted to be an investment banker, and there was a recruiting event coming up. She said she didn't like going to these things alone, and asked if I'd go with her. I said sure; I had no desire to be an investment banker, but consulting companies would also be attending, so I could talk with them. However, the way it works is that you put your name forward first and then you're picked by particular companies. Wouldn't you know it: Smith Barney — an investment bank — asked me for an interview.

"JUST BEING YOURSELF AND GETTING INTO THE TRENCHES GOES A LONG WAY TOWARD MAKING OTHERS FEEL VALUED."

—Lindsay Sacknoff

A senior partner interviewed me. She seemed great, although I was nervous. It was going well, but at one point she said, "Lindsay, why do you want to be an investment banker?" The first thing that came out of my 21-year-old mouth was, "I don't *know* if I want to be an investment banker."

She looked surprised, but we kept going with the interview. I did get a call back the next morning. Typically, the calls come from the recruiter, but it was the senior partner herself on the other end of the phone. "I wanted you to know that we're not going to take this to the next level," she said, "but you really impressed me with your honesty in answering that question. And I wanted to tell you that if you don't want to be an investment banker, you shouldn't be one. If you do something you enjoy, I know you'll do really well." I'll always remember this senior woman's kindness and willingness to share her honesty and advice.

THE MOMENT

From that moment I've self-identified as authentic
and honest, and to this day, I am who I am.

From that moment I've self-identified as authentic and honest, and to this day, I am who I am. It allows me to connect with people better. Here's a recent example of how being authentic is good for the whole team. Not long ago, when I was a couple of months into my current job — part of which is running our call centres in the U.S. — we'd just gone through a major change in the technology that supports our online banking. Whenever customers experience a change in what they're accustomed to using, we get a higher than usual number of people contacting our call centres for help. We expected that to be the case for two to three days. But by the time we were two or three weeks in, the call centre teams were in crisis-management mode trying to keep up with the workload.

I felt I needed to get out to the different sites — Maine, South Carolina, and New Jersey — and hear what this kind of workload feels like to the person answering the phone.

Each call centre has a couple of hundred people working the phones, and at each one I pulled together teams of 10 to 15 and explained that I wanted their feedback. I heard things like, "It's hard on our families because we're working long hours, and it's tough to shut off and be there for them when we get home late." Just making those direct connections helped build morale — some said, "Wow, you came to visit us, you really care" — but we had to do something for them.

So we helped people get off the phones more. We gave them more breaks to do other types of work, we hired more people, and we gave them thank-you bonuses for all the extra time. We had TD executives go see them. In one call centre, our head of distribution went from desk to desk handing out soft pretzels with mustard smiley faces on them. Little gestures like that helped alleviate some of the tension. Our head of HR in Maine had a golden retriever breeder bring some puppies to the call centre for a visit. Holding a puppy is a great stress reliever. It was all emotionally powerful, and a lot of fun.

These efforts not only helped the call centre employees cope; we published photos on our company intranet once we got through that difficult phase, and the whole company was talking about it. Folks remembered the fun but also how hard they worked, and were now walking taller; they'd gone into battle together and come out of it together. I've learned that just being yourself and getting into the trenches goes a long way toward making others feel valued. Ultimately, everyone wins.

PART THREE

The Judy Project

*I*t took crazy ambition in a moment of profound grief for a group of friends to create a new kind of women's leadership program that would reflect the admirable qualities of the friend they had just lost. It wasn't the idea that was so crazy. People come up with ideas all the time. The remarkable part was to turn that idea into a well-funded, professionally supported, weeklong program, a unique initiative to support women who are on track to C-suite jobs. Oh yes, and to accomplish all this in less than one year.

Coming Together

T he Judy Project began at a bar, where Colleen Moorehead and Lorna Borenstein were commiserating after a harrowing visit to the funeral home where friends and family were reeling from the shock of Judy's sudden death in late March 2002. At the time, Colleen was president of E★TRADE Canada; Lorna was president of eBay Canada. They wanted to seize the moment and secure Judy's legacy. It was critical to them to keep alive her important ideas and leadership voice. They felt passionately that other women needed to hear about Judy's ideas, to know her impact, and to learn from her examples. So they reached out to Judy's friends.

"When Colleen and Lorna called to say they wanted to do something in Judy's memory, it almost sounded like a foreign language," says Janet Kestin, one of Judy's closest friends and then co-creative director at ad agency Ogilvy & Mather Canada. "We were all truly in shock. The 'clan,' our close-knit group of friends — more like family, really — was focused on getting through each day, trying to keep Judy's family and each other afloat. How could we possibly contribute to something outside when we were so focused on shoring up the inside? I couldn't imagine it."

But under Colleen's direction, what started as a notion quickly gathered steam. Funders stepped up without hesitation. The first call was, logically, to Microsoft, Judy's employer, where Colleen found an open response from CEO Frank Clegg. He'd already decided that the company would do something as long as it had the support of Judy's partner, David Powell. Initial thoughts included a chair at a university, but that was dismissed, as it was neither original nor spoke to Judy's uniqueness. No, a legacy demanded more. With David fully supporting the idea of some kind of leadership program, Microsoft donated $250,000 and the project was born.

Colleen, Lorna, and Cathy Preston, president of Preston Human Capital Group, began knocking on doors to secure more sponsors. CIBC was an early supporter, and that encouraged other financial institutions to join in. Deloitte stepped up, as did other professional-services companies and law firms. Frank Clegg brought Bell and Rogers into the fold. Ogilvy & Mather, Judy's past employer, encouraged other marketers and advertising agencies to contribute. Every large organization where women filled the management ranks was targeted, and, ultimately, the launch was supported by organizations across multiple sectors. Within four months, contributions grew to over $700,000.

By then, the steering committee consisted of Colleen and Lorna, Cathy, David, Janet, and Daryl Aitken, then an executive at eBay Canada, as well as Paula Knight, director of communications at Microsoft Canada, Bukurie Kulla, from the advertising world, Janice Rubin, the senior partner of law firm Rubin Tomlinson LLP, Anne Sutherland, head of Planning Ahead, a strategic planning consultancy, and Judith Wright, then assistant deputy minister of Strategic Planning and Policy at the Ontario Ministry of Education. "It was a mash-up of family, friends, and colleagues who had a strong desire to pay forward Judy's extraordinary way of thinking and being, and her desire to bring more women leaders into the world," Janet says. "The group was mostly smart women, and David: thoughtful, kind, shattered, parsing what felt true and what didn't. Everyone believed there was something special, a little magic, in Judy's leadership style."

They knew it was time to diversify. There was a sense of urgency — the team needed to capitalize on the interest in the moment. It wasn't hard to find people willing to join the cause. "Judy had a funeral and two big memorials," Daryl notes, "so we had a big network to draw on."

At only the second steering committee meeting, Colleen suggested that the group needed a big-name partner, tapping the University of Toronto's Rotman School of Management as the preferred candidate. Colleen proposed a meeting with Rotman's dean, Roger Martin. As she put it, "We have to start at the top."

It paid off; Martin was very helpful and encouraging. He laid out the options Rotman could offer and set goals for the steering committee. From May to December 2002, the committee met every two weeks to debate the core content. Corporate leaders were consulted, executive surveys conducted, and the concept and principles of a leadership forum emerged.

In September 2002 the steering committee's proposals were presented to Rotman, and were well received. The committee was expanded to include Rotman representatives Geeta Sheker (still leading the program today), Ariana Bradford, and the inaugural academic co-director, professor Brian Golden, then associate professor of Strategic Management and Organization.

The next stage of planning began with a formal presentation by Rotman of a more detailed program. It embraced the goal that the steering committee had articulated — to build stronger business organizations through the advancement of more women into senior leadership positions. The focus is on equipping senior women executives so that they may better navigate to the upper reaches of corporations. The objective is to address the realities of the challenges women face in seeking to be leaders of large organizations.

Before partnering, it was critical to ensure Rotman understood that the steering committee was a partner, and that the team wouldn't simply hand over the basic ideas and money for Rotman to run the program on its own. The Judy Project was, and remains, a true collaboration, which is key to the program's remaining faithful to the original underlying principles.

From the beginning, the curriculum guide was Judy's breakfast speech.

To represent Judy, the curriculum needed to acknowledge the whole person, not just one's business and work life. Judy was an example of living a full life as a leader, wife, mother, mentor, and friend. Additionally, the program needed to be an open dialogue on the issues facing women as well as a guide on how to thrive regardless of the existing system. This would replicate Judy's role as a wise mentor in so many women's lives.

The content needed to be as insightful and multifaceted as she was. Judy was both book smart and practical smart, a creative thinker with a high EQ and a collaborative style, a communicator with vision, and an experienced executive with a breadth of business perspective to share.

The program could have wound up with a dry, uninspiring name. But the committee wanted every aspect to reflect its heart: Judy.

"The name — The Judy Project, an Enlightened Leadership Forum for Executive Women — highlights the differences from a lot of other women's leadership initiatives," Daryl says. "It addresses the whole person because it was inspired by a whole person." Judy's own words inspired the committee to create content not found in other executive programs. For instance, research showed that women were more reluctant than men to take credit for success, or even to state a position at a meeting, so the committee thought it was important to encourage women to own their success and take credit for their leading accomplishments.

To address these kinds of issues, it was clear that The Judy Project would need a new approach. The committee put everything on the table — judo, lessons on power dynamics, drama coaching to find one's voice, a cooking class. Not every new idea succeeded (judo was discontinued after year one), but the innovative spirit inspired the team to push the boundaries and get to a unique content that would resonate with all participants.

The official public announcement to corporate sponsors and the media took place at Rotman in December 2002. The first weeklong retreat session was mounted in April 2003, less than 12 months after the first steering committee meeting and 13 months after Judy's death. It was proof that the steering committee and its Rotman partners had channelled Judy's mantra: "getting stuff done, having an impact, making a difference, and accomplishing what others thought not possible."

***

After more than 15 years, The Judy Project helps women to be their best, authentic self and to harness their strengths. They learn to visualize their leadership attributes against their most admired leader. They gain a clear view of their network, and the unconscious bias that may be holding them back. They create their brand and learn how to build a successful and sustainable plan to stay in the game by forming a personal advisory board with other Judy Project participants.

The group cooking class has become a cherished tradition at The Judy Project. The annual Tuscan meal inspired by Judy's speech is something that celebrity chef Christine Cushing leads and looks forward to attending every year.

There are among the many elements of The Judy Project that make it both unique and ambitious:

- The leadership is shared between the academic and business co-directors.

- Active CEOs participate each year, sharing current stories of leadership.

- There is a focus on developing senior leaders with a potential for C-suite positions in five to seven years.

- Participants join long-term personal advisory boards in order to sustain their leadership ambition, since The Judy Project isn't just about the now; it's about the rest of each participant's career.

Judy's style of leadership lives on, not only in the weeklong leadership program but also in the hundreds of women who have graduated from it. These women have carried their new leadership lessons back into the workplace. It has changed them, and the people around them.

Staying In

Sustaining Ambition

At the end of the weeklong Judy Project program, participants are divided into personal advisory boards (PABs) of about seven women each — an effective way to enable continued sharing among group members. The diversity of each group is important, since this can leverage best practice across sectors, experience levels, and perspectives (and so, for example, those who work for companies that are direct competitors won't be on the same PAB).

A PAB isn't a social group. It's an element of the program developed to sustain participants over the long term by offering a trusted circle of peers who understand you, your ambitions, and your goals. You could think of the group as a personal board of directors, a curated collection of high-functioning directors offering opinions on the business of "Me Corp."

Their meetings aren't optional; those who miss two consecutive sessions will no longer be a PAB member. Some PABs — including Geeta Sheker's — continue for many years. Others last just a couple of years. But the results indicate that for their commitment, participants get lots of return.

Essential ingredients of a PAB include confidentiality, diversity, and commitment. It's basically a caring group of committed peers and friends who meet regularly to discuss both business and personal issues. There should be an environment of mutual trust and integrity, where members are truthful with each other, offer and receive counsel, promote and encourage self-accountability, and point out blind spots. Meetings and retreats combine presentations, discussions, celebrations, and pure fun.

Anyone can go away for a one-week program, and it can be the best learning week you've ever had. But something has to sustain you. The PAB is that sustaining piece. It's "the north star of your goals." It links you back, says Colleen Moorehead, to all those aspirations you had for yourself during The Judy Project week — and connects you, on an ongoing basis, to the people you shared that week with. "Your PAB is like the best kind of board of directors: strong, wise, knowledgeable, and building on your strengths. It's part of the success metric."

Inside a Personal Advisory Board
How It Works, What You Learn, Why It's So Important

Here we consider one particular PAB, the first one formed at The Judy Project, in 2004. Originally made up of 10 members, for the past 12 years it has been the same amazing group of seven. A few women in this group knew each other before the PAB formed, or had mutual friends. But the close, strong relationships that have since been collectively forged have become essential to each one of these women.

What follows is a freewheeling roundtable chat with most of this first PAB's members:

Clare Gaudet, Vice President and Chief Anti–Money Laundering Officer, National Bank of Canada

Daryl Aitken, Owner, Fabric Spark; Director,
Torstar Corporation

Stacey Grant-Thompson, Chief Marketing Officer,
Manulife Financial Corporation

Sandra Sanderson, Senior Vice President, Marketing,
Sobeys Inc.; former Chief Marketing Officer, Walmart Canada

Susan Ross, Partner, ISM Access

Geeta Sheker, Co-Founder and Director, University of
Toronto Rotman School of Management's Initiative for
Women in Business

Clare Gaudet: If you think about how small corporate Canada
is, if there are six degrees of separation, then definitely many of us
are going to be connected — especially because we're women in
corporate Canada! We're probably only one to two degrees away
from each other. You'd think we would form close relationships
with each other, but that doesn't always happen.

Daryl Aitken: You don't naturally have deep connections
with other people professionally. I have a good friend in finance
at eBay because I worked there, but I have a marketing background, so I don't know many people from the worlds of
finance and law and education. The amazing thing about a PAB
is that you get a chance to be exposed to different points of
view in an intimate way.

Clare: In our PAB a lot of us have a marketing background. I'm
a lawyer, and sometimes I'd like a redo and go into marketing!
Judy said that if women are to advance, they tend to move around.
People gain different industry experiences as they evolve their
careers, and that's very valuable. In our PAB, lots of changes have

happened. There are only two of us who are still with the organizations we were with when we started. Among us, we have different insights. I'm a big believer in hearing different perspectives — a "walk a mile in my shoes" approach — because you get a better perspective when you can see the view from the other side.

Stacey Grant-Thompson: And the thing is, in our PAB we don't discuss things specific to marketing or any one industry; we talk about leadership, opportunities, broader functions — not the particular one you're in. What we discuss here is more along the lines of a business performance challenge, or a team challenge.

Sandra Sanderson: I've moved companies several times since our PAB started, and in the time we've been together I've appreciated using our PAB as a sounding board for making decisions with my eyes wide open.

Susan Ross: We often talk about where we are in our personal lives, too, so the confidentiality is a huge factor. There is trust. You don't get that same feeling when you're sharing things with friends; behind their reaction may be the desire to please you, to tell you what they think you want to hear. But here, along with the trust you also get the cold, hard truth.

Clare: You also have a caring environment. We all care about each other; bearing witness to each other's lives is so important. No one around this table has an "agenda."

Stacey: You just know these people want the best for you; they've known you a long time, so there's a core encouragement for trying to do your best. You get a cushion that helps buoy you when things aren't going that well. With the PAB you're always moving forward, you're always setting goals, you always want to improve.

Geeta Sheker: There's trust, confidentiality, constructive feedback, instructive insights … everyone wants the best for you — and at the same time will call you on your blind spots.

Daryl: Yes, we've often said, "Don't do that, it's not a good idea." How many of us have friends who will tell us what we're really like? So when we bring an issue up, the women here tell you that you need to face it. There's no other relationship in your life that can do that for you.

Stacey: We all have professional expertise, we share the core base of The Judy Project learnings, we have well-rounded leadership backgrounds, and we have our PAB's continuity. We've all become close friends, but it's not the same as other friends; it's in a different category. The core is a professional relationship that is just … different. It's not the same as the girls you go on a girls' weekend with.

Daryl: We're here to help each other. We don't drink together, by the way; there's no alcohol at our meetings — well, okay, sometimes we drink together *[laughter]*.

Susan: Yes, we do let loose on our annual retreats.

Sandra: I see them as team building, but without the cheesy corporate team-building exercises, like walking ropes. They bring us even closer together, and that helps us to stay connected.

Stacey: We have an incredible shorthand for how we get on together. On our early retreats we had specific exercises to talk about what mattered to each of us, and we worked through that content over many years to get us a baseline.

Daryl: As far as our PAB meetings, the structure was consistent in the first two to three years; we were quite disciplined about it. It got us into good habits. But then we evolved the format to what suited us better as a group.

Geeta: The discipline of meeting regularly has helped us survive. I know other PABs who didn't do that from the start, and they didn't last. For us it's become an intrinsic part of our lives. We look forward to it, and we miss it when we can't be there. It's so interesting. We want to hear how everyone is doing.

Stacey: The biggest thing for me is the advice. If I'm struggling with anything professional, I consult the group for perspective. I know I'm going to get multiple views, and I can leverage it. The advice is central; it helps me avoid falling into a trap because of my blind spots. There's that extra support that says you can do it, be brave. This group is good about encouraging you to go after the bold thing, and that you deserve it. And generally we all deserve *a lot*.

Daryl: We tell each other to be even bolder than you think you should be.

Stacey: Yes, we can see when someone is holding back. We say, "You deserve that promotion." Or: "You *should* change that person on your team." It's sometimes a validation of ideas, and it makes you more comfortable in your choices.

Daryl: We have a lot of ambition for each other — personally, professionally, how we see each other. I can think of a specific incident when Sandra and I were doing some planning: she pushed my thinking, and I came home with a to-do list. Because she had more ambition for me than I saw for myself.

Sandra: I've been so inspired by all of you. I've learned more about myself just from the way I hear you talking about your lives. Susan, I'm so inspired by you moving to your chapter two, to a new life, and when I hear your updates I think, *I want to be able to do that one day.*

Susan: I moved out of the corporate world. I'm now teaching, doing non-profit board work, and taking up new interests, like golfing.

Daryl: And your eyes light up when you're talking about teaching!

Susan: It's a self-actualization. I feel like I'm out there doing things that are fulfilling in a whole different way.

Geeta: We talk about ambition — the seed of The Judy Project — and we do have that. Without The Judy Project and this PAB, I wouldn't have had the initiative to launch the Women in Business course at Rotman. I took a leap of faith, and it was the collective ambition of everyone that helped me to push forward.

Susan: It's like a workshop, a chance to talk out an idea and try it on for size.

Clare: The quality of the decision making is very thoughtful. You don't avoid certain topics. The corporate world can be tough, and not everyone is ambitious for your success. One could argue that maybe you'd have made the same decisions without your PAB, but your PAB provides you with a trusted sounding board that affirms and often completes your decision making. In a way it gives you a secret advantage over other folks. If you're going through a tough patch, the answer to "Who you gonna call?" is that you have a team to call on.

Daryl: I'm certain I would have made worse decisions in my career, no question, if not for this PAB. It's not only the chance to come in with specific things to discuss, it's everything over the years — this level of discourse from so many points of view on issues that are pretty global, things like career management, organizational problems, elder care.

Stacey: Through our PAB we get nuggets, pieces of wisdom that make your life better: books, music, places to travel, parenting tips, how you look after parents. People sharing ideas for the best of things, and the challenges, and you just soak them all up.

Clare: We bring our whole lives here. We're not just talking about professional challenges; it's our whole lives. Yes, we do regular updates, and "explorations," which is talking in-depth about an issue. We do have discipline in our PAB; you maintain that through sweat equity: we made a promise to each other and we follow through. We're committed to what we've built together. That saying, "It's in giving that you receive" — this group is very much about that.

Stacey: It's like personal coaching without the expense.

Daryl: Just hearing what others say about someone else's problem, you learn so much. It's an amazing bit of exposure.

Clare: I was reflecting on that. I realize I've had the most amazing teachers and coaches in our PAB. There are things I'd never thought about before, and just listening to the interactions in the PAB has taught me to consider an issue in different ways, and it's made me a better person.

Stacey: You're gaining experience for situations before you even need it. If you've heard about a situation thanks to the PAB, and then you have to face it, you feel like you know what it's like to face it. For sure I'm a much better leader than I would be without that.

Sandra: When you're really close to your own situation you can't see the forest for the trees. Having a balcony view thanks to your PAB helps.

Susan: I can think of a situation when I got advice for dealing with a colleague, and boy was it good, it really worked. You get clarity.

Daryl: There was an incident when I would have done something else if not for our talking it through. When we do an exploration, the questions are so good. It's hard to imagine how you'd do it without this exposure at our PAB.

Stacey: To explain a bit about how explorations work, sometimes during our regular updates at meetings, a member might say, "You should do an exploration on that." It's usually about a big and meaty situation, something you're wrestling with and need the group's help with. Maybe it's organizational changes, political dynamics in terms of colleagues, and you're trying to figure out how to set yourself up for the best outcome. You do your own thinking on it first and make sure everyone gets the context. Sometimes you've gone as far as proposing solutions. Then everyone on the PAB asks you to clarify a few things, and then they provide advice on a course of action.

Daryl: And it's not always academic; you might not have done any research. It's about needing to hear other perspectives, to ask yourself, *Have I thought of everything?* We talk about people dynamics a lot, negotiating the challenges of many personality types. The PAB can help if you want to test your script, play through a scene to prepare for a meeting.

Geeta: Some PABs have had to take on new members because they've lost some; sometimes, two PABs merge into one. Early on we discussed whether we should let new people into our group, and we decided it would erode trust if we did that.

Susan: We have roles. Stacey is treasurer for life. We'll pool money to have dinner together at our meetings, sometimes a holiday dinner, and then there's the retreat.

Clare: Where alcohol is consumed.

Daryl: We're not teetotallers!

Stacey: The chair manages the agenda and the schedule, and someone manages the retreat. We move that around.

Sandra: I want you to come to Florida!

Stacey: It's interesting how it's changed over the years. Denise is now in New York, Sam is in Florida, Clare was in Montreal. Yet we still managed to make it work.

Geeta: We've never deviated from the substance of what the PAB set out to do. We do a review annually, at the retreat, to see how things are going, maybe change it up, maybe one aspect isn't working.

Daryl: All of us have spoken at The Judy Project about how valuable a PAB is. I for one can't imagine investing the time in attending The Judy Project and then have it just stop. That week is amazing, and it gives you a lift. It's a really immersive experience, with smart, accomplished women, and if you didn't have any way to thread the experience from there — i.e., through a PAB — it would inevitably fade, because life takes over. So a PAB is a spectacular way to keep your exposure to The Judy Project integrated in your life, to keep its energy alive.

Stacey: With the PAB, you just keep advancing.

Clare: It's nurturing.

Susan: If The Judy Project is the planting of the seed, then the PAB is the farming and the harvest.

Daryl: It's the best thing to come out of The Judy Project, without question. The Judy Project is just the beginning.

Jane Kinney

VICE CHAIR, DELOITTE LLP

"The Sisters"

The best thing that came out of my time at The Judy Project was the PAB I formed with six other women. Our PAB has been going strong now for 12 years. During that time we've been through many ups and downs, both personally and professionally. The mutual support of our group has had a lasting impact on each of us.

When we first formed our PAB, we followed the rigid rules that are standard for PABs, such as if you missed two meetings in one year, you were out. Rules like these certainly have value, and they work for many PABs, but what worked for us was tossing out the rules. We have a business agenda, but we also have fun. We have a standing meeting each month, on a Friday at 7 a.m., and go on a retreat together each year — last year's retreat was in Barbados, where one of our PAB members now lives. We have a 100 percent attendance rate at the retreats, by the way!

Our first retreat, in 2006, was at Langdon Hall, a hotel and spa in Ontario. We didn't know each other that well, but we sure did after that weekend, partly because one of our group, Anne Sutherland, had some exercises she wanted us all to do. One was called the Lifeline exercise, which featured a grid on which we each plotted lines to indicate the quality of three aspects of our lives — personal, financial, and professional — from childhood to present. It really opened my eyes, because at the time my career was going very well but my personal life was a disaster. My marriage was breaking down, and I hadn't actually confided that to anyone — not my lifelong friends, not my family … nobody.

I ended up sharing everything that weekend with a group of women I barely knew. Then others started sharing. It was so emotional and impactful, and created an incredible bond between us. That was the start of our utter transparency together, and our discretion; we always maintain a cone of silence around everything we discuss.

At our retreat two years ago in Montreal, we did the same exercise. This was 10 years after the first one, and we tallied two divorces, three marriages, two moves, and many career transitions in that time. These were big changes that we've all shared in deeply over the years.

When we started out, we all had in mind the goal set by The Judy Project: to be CEOs within five years. None of us have made it, though we've all had the potential. There are perhaps two out of our seven who still have a shot. But what we've created together over the years is more important than that. Whenever one of us has an important decision to make or a sticky issue to resolve, we all jump on a call to discuss it. We know each other so well, and we know each other's environments; as a result, we can listen objectively and provide strong advice. We refer to each other as "The Sisters." None of us are friends separately; we're always connected only as a group. The experience has been nothing short of amazing.

Sustaining Ambition

If you're feeling inspired after reading the stories of those who've attended The Judy Project, here's how it has paved the way for other women's leadership development programs — and has truly been a catalyst for change.

Geeta Sheker

CO-FOUNDER AND DIRECTOR, ROTMAN SCHOOL OF MANAGEMENT'S INITIATIVE FOR WOMEN IN BUSINESS; OVERSAW THE 2003 LAUNCH OF THE JUDY PROJECT

Learning at All Levels

The Judy Project is designed for women in senior roles as they consider and prepare for reaching the most senior role in their organization. Given the criteria for attendance, it remains quite an intimate group each year — just 25 to 30 participants. After it began in 2003, many Judy Project alumnae and sponsors asked if we'd considered a similar program for women at other levels. We also heard repeatedly from our participants that they wish there'd been a program like The Judy Project earlier in their careers.

Based on all that feedback, it became apparent that more programs were needed for women at all levels in the organization. In this way The Judy Project led to a broader portfolio of executive women's courses at Rotman, where in 2008 the Initiative for Women in Business was launched. Its aim is to keep the corporate pipeline filled with talented women. Today, this initiative offers seven programs that meet the specific needs of professional women, ranging from those early in their careers to those aspiring to C-suite positions. Here are some examples:

- The Emerging Leaders program helps women make the transition from manager to leader, broaden their leadership capacity, and equip them for increased responsibility.

- The Athena program is for women early in their careers. It provides leadership training and effective strategies for performance and career management.

- The Back to Work program supports women who want to re-enter the workforce after having taken a career break of many years.

Over the past 16 years, Judy Project alumnae have supported both The Judy Project and the Initiative for Women in Business by sending women from their own companies to participate and by sponsoring specific programs. That was the case when the law firms Blakes, Osler, and McCarthy, all Judy Project founding sponsors, came together to sponsor Business Leadership for Women Lawyers, a program designed to retain and advance women at law firms' associate and income partner levels.

Beatrix Dart

CO-FOUNDER AND EXECUTIVE DIRECTOR, ROTMAN SCHOOL OF MANAGEMENT'S
INITIATIVE FOR WOMEN IN BUSINESS; PROFESSOR OF STRATEGIC MANAGEMENT;
STEERING COMMITTEE CHAIR, 30% CLUB CANADA

A Legacy of Success

What's unique about The Judy Project is the legacy impact: its participants, along with any others who've been touched by the project, share a passion for paying forward the mission for gender diversity at all levels of corporate leadership.

An important goal for Rotman's Initiative for Women in Business has been to ensure that women have the opportunity to serve in decision-making roles, including corporate board roles. Progress is being made to that end through efforts like the 30% Club Canada, a campaign that was born in the U.K. in 2010, at a time when only 12 percent of board positions were being filled by women. It initially focused on engaging the chairs of corporate boards to change their boards' composition. And it had tremendous success: the number of women on boards in the U.K. now stands at 29 percent.

The Canadian chapter started in 2015. Since then, the percentage of women on corporate boards has risen from 14 to 22 percent, which is progress in the right direction — but still slow going. The aim is to reach 30 percent (hence the name) by 2022.

We feel privileged to be making an impact on gender equality across Canada, to be pushing the envelope on gender leadership by helping advance women at all stages of their career. The Rotman Initiative for Women in Business plays an integral role in supporting the corporate and public sectors with thought leadership and hands-on, practical approaches. Judy Elder would have been proud of her legacy.

Judy's Speech

Women's Television Network — Gift of Wisdom Series
Insightful strategies from winning women

*Judy Elder, General Manager,
Consumer Products Division,
Microsoft Canada;
Chair, Canadian Marketing
Association*

March 7, 2002

*Board of Trade of
Metropolitan Toronto*

Good morning and thank you for joining us today. I must say, I find the 7:30 start particularly ambitious for me, and probably for a few evening people in the audience. Why is it that we always admire morning people? Like it's the only virtue, as in the apologetic "I'm not a morning person." Why isn't being an evening person just as virtuous? Anyway, for those of you who are evening people, thanks for getting up; for those morning people in the audience, well I suppose there are other things which don't come easy to you.

That's a bit of a segue into my theme this morning, because I want to talk about ambition. Freely, frankly, and nonjudgmentally. Which is not often the way ambition is thought about when used

219

adjectivally with women. Somehow "ambitious" is right up there with "aggressive" when it comes to linkage with the B-word.

I want to start with a story, a girls' week away story. And by the way, for those of you with careers, partners, kids, dogs, employees — there is no better stress reliever and no harder plan to execute than a girls' week away. Those of you who have experienced this singularly selfish pleasure will no doubt corroborate my conclusion. I'm not talking weekend, which is good; I'm advocating week, which is infinitely better.

Anyway, this story is true and it came to be a life-altering experience in self-awareness, certainly for me, and I suspect also for the friends I shared it with. The title of this talk is stolen directly from this tale, hence the slightly pretentious "Mothers, Fathers, Men, Ambition."

Imagine, if you will, six 30- and 40-something women rendezvousing at the Villa Mimosa, a gloriously secluded villa in the hills outside Lucca, in a splendid Tuscan September. We'd managed to leave behind the jobs, husbands, kids starting school that week, parents, at least six crises of monumental proportion. Five of us came from Toronto, one from Germany. Only a couple of us worked together, one of us didn't even really know the majority. Pulling this trip off was so miraculous given our many commitments and guilts that, try as we might, we haven't ever been able to repeat it, and we've been trying for five years.

As we pull into the villa, fig tree in full fruit, surrounded by olive groves, a rosemary bush the size of a Christmas tree, a perfect swimming pool immaculately maintained, we are graciously greeted by the extremely elegant landlady, dressed for villa renting in some amazingly understated Armani-type skirt-blouse-scarf combo. We, of course, look like typical North American schlubs without so much as a smear of lipstick. The contessa, after spotting at least three wedding rings in the crowd, and despite her normal discretion, can't help but inquire of us, "How come, six female?" We stumbled to explain *"amiche, amiche, si?"* — but I think she was unconvinced!

We arrived in the afternoon, well provisioned with food, sunscreen, and much wine, and discovered to our delight that the place sported a well-equipped kitchen, an outdoor Italian-style barbecue, and a massive hearth in front of the expansive dining room table. After a swim and a few sips, we set about the challenge of preparing dinner. With six self-described keen cooks, we had lots to do and plenty of time to do it, and plenty of wine. Dinner prep seemed to take a few hours, and dinner consumption a few hours more, with the commensurate number of dead soldiers and wicked first-night hangovers the next morning.

Clearly, in order to avoid certain cirrhosis, we needed a more organized and formal structure to give shape and purpose to the long fragrant evenings at Villa Mimosa. The notion of a topic a night was born, and we quickly declared the topics, one per night, to be "Fathers, Mothers, Men, Ambition." The goal was really quite simple: to inspire the intellects and personalities around the table to discuss those who have impacted our lives, relationships, and potentially why we were where we were at that point in time. Who knew at the time the discussions would be so cathartic, so revealing or so memorable, but so they proved to be.

So, Evening 1, we discuss "Mothers," lots of good stuff, lots of "you think you had it rough," lots of admissions of friendship out the other side, a little continuing dissatisfaction, the usual stuff, netting out that we have all pretty much resolved and reached resolution with our mothers over the past 30-odd years.

Evening 2 — "Fathers." All in all, less meat on that bone, with a couple of notable exceptions and concluding ultimately that they did have influence, were role models, and applied pressure on our lives. Go figure.

Evening 3 — "Men." Need I say more, lots to say and share … and all of it volunteered with enthusiasm and much of it recognized as not unique!

And then we came to our final topic — "Ambition."

Now by this point you might have thought that we had this down pat — a terrific menu, a cooking team working like a well-oiled machine, and a highly satisfactory way of enjoying interesting, controversial conversation, opinion, insight, and just a healthy amount of self-absorption. Well, when I — I think it was me — reminded us of the topic, we have the dinner table equivalent of staring at your shoes. No spontaneous examples, no freely volunteered opinion, just nervous giggling — nervous giggling *for chrissake*, from six professional, successful, accomplished women!

So I take the plunge and confess to a lifetime of being ambitious, of never being satisfied with where I was today, of always wanting the next job up, of wanting to be in charge and being convinced I could do a fine job of it. I bare my soul, and they stare at me open-mouthed. Admiring my courage, as I'm later told.

But, Chianti Classico being a superb lubricant, others gradually share this most personal of confessions, some admitting that this is the first occasion they have ever knowingly acknowledged what was readily apparent — that we are all ambitious, our success to that point impossible without the driving force of ambition pushing us to compete, to contribute, to sustain a healthy and ongoing dissatisfaction with the status quo as far as our own lives are concerned.

Evening 4 ultimately proves to be the most revealing, the most confessional and, in my view, the most inspiring of all the evening discussions we had. Certainly, there was no new topic for Evening 5.

This story does have a twist at the ending, which I will share with you later on, but I think it is a superb and personal example of the issue behind my theme today. "Ambition," unlike other subjects like "Leadership," "Mentoring," "Breaking Through," is a pretty loaded word. I'd like to explore the importance and nature of ambition a little bit, and share my perspective on this absolutely essential ingredient to success.

At the time of this Italian adventure, I was 43, president of OgilvyOne, a large and successful direct marketing agency. I had two sons, a divorce, a new partner, a beautiful home, a 70-person-plus payroll to meet, parents, siblings, nieces and nephews, happy clients, and clearly fabulous friends. Since, I've left the agency business, spent two years with IBM in a senior North American job, left that company to tackle another challenge at Microsoft (a company where some days I feel as old as Methuselah), and spent the last two years building a team and a huge growth machine within the consumer group at Microsoft. Something that has me working harder and longer than I've worked in years.

As an aside, as those of you will know who have joined companies in a senior capacity, the irony of it is that you are recruited for your track record elsewhere, and the moment you're inside the company all credit for past success vanishes and you are only as good as what you've done for the new team, which of course is nothing on day one. Now back to "ambition."

Why did I leave a secure and comfortable post at the virtual top of an industry I'd been climbing for 18 years? And by the way, it wasn't the money. It was two things: boredom and thwarted ambition. Two sides of the same coin. After all, isn't "ambition" just a more focused word for "motivation"?

I badly wanted and was ready for the next steep bit of the learning curve — and I wasn't going to get it where I was. So I took the plunge into a new industry, a new company, and a whole new set of evaluation criteria. Maybe a crazy tradeoff in terms of balance, competency, even top job potential, but completely satisfying and stimulating from a lifelong journey perspective. And, when that experience failed to meet all the expectations my ambition put on it, I switched again — back to a line job — and began the learning curve all over again.

The thing about ambition, for me anyway, is that it's not about the destination, it's about the journey. And as long as I'm always doing more, stretching harder, not being bored (a key component for me), then I'm realizing today's ambition.

As I've thought more about women and their ambition, I've come to the conclusion that, in our society's eyes, there are two sorts of ambition. First, and most applauded, is the desire for personal best — in sports, the arts, science, the professions. From this kind of ambition we get our Olympians, our Margaret Atwoods, our Beverley McLachlins. Women do extremely well in areas of individual achievement.

But when it comes to organizational ambition, the passionate desire to lead complex organizations in business, government, and the public sector, we do far worse. The representation of women in officer roles in corporate Canada is a pathetic 6.4 percent of line jobs. We hold only 3 percent of clout titles — Chief Executive something titles.

When MP Dr. Carolyn Bennett challenged the shocking gender imbalance of cabinet, not only did our prime minister virtually ignore her comment, her colleagues subsequently voted her out of her caucus position.

In the *Maclean's* magazine recent list of the 50 most influential Canadians, only nine women appear at all. And of those, only four, Anne McLellan, the justice minister; Nellie Cournoyea, the chairwoman of the Inuvialuit Regional Corporation; Martha Piper, president of UBC; and Louise Comeau, head of the Federation of Regional Municipalities, can be said to hold organizational influence rather than influence as a result of personal achievement. Not much of a list, despite these admirable women.

Why is this so? Why are we celebrated for personal best but, dare I say it, blocked from organizational top-dog positions? Maybe because while women may be personally trusted, they are *less trusted to lead us.* We don't have *alpha people,* we have *alpha males.* When it comes down to picking someone who is going to win for us, we are inclined to pick the big strong competitive, undistracted, *yes,* ruthless guy. Personally, I think it's unlikely that the Packard family would be putting up such a fuss if Carly Fiorina was a Carl!

And this brings me to one of the best pieces of advice I was ever given. An early boss and longtime mentor told me once that "people never get anywhere unless someone wants them to." Translation: Organizational ambition requires that others be ambitious for you.

In my case I've been extremely lucky in my parents, my partner, even my kids. All are ambitious for me; in fact my husband frequently embarrasses me by sending any and all newspaper mentions of me to an extensive mailing list of friends and relatives. I'm not sure you have to have an actively supportive and helpful spouse, but for sure, if there's a daily guilt trip going on about your divided attention, no inner drive can sustain you and the marriage alike.

Equally important are the people you work with and for, and those who work for you. Organizations are political; people quite naturally operate on the "what's in it for me?" factor: enlightened self-interest. If they are ambitious for you it will be because they believe in your ability to help them achieve their goals. When people are prepared to go on dangerous missions with you, you know they're ambitious for you because they see you as helping them win. Think of all the jerks who get ahead organizationally (the Enron leadership comes to mind). The reason they do so is because they bring others along with them.

I happen to believe that if you win for others along with yourself you will be rewarded with ongoing support and loyalty, and that loyalty will transfer from organization to organization, whether by reputation or, the truly to be cherished, people willing to follow you to other places. And by the way, I don't believe you need to be a jerk to get ahead; in my experience, most jerks eventually get their comeuppance.

My first personal heroine was Queen Elizabeth the First. I still voraciously consume everything written about her. Talk about the "Mothers, Fathers, Men, Ambition" quadrangle: boy did she have them all.

Born to her dad's second wife, and first beheaded wife, not only does she survive and thrive in the political intrigue of sixteenth-century England, once she finally gets the corner office she's got religious upheaval and the *freakin'* Spanish Armada to deal with. Not to mention a whole slew of ambitious men who want to bed her or marry her for their own ends.

I think what I admire most about her is that she recognized early on that it wasn't about getting somewhere for herself alone. It was about using her superior skills, understanding, and vision to take the whole country forward, and doing so meant a life-long balancing act. The result was she gave her name to an age, an age in which the accomplishments of others really defined the achievements.

It's no accident that I stuck on Elizabeth as a heroine early on. I clearly wasn't going to be an athlete, or an artist, and I've always envied those who knew from an early age that they were born to be an astronaut, or a doctor. I'm still waiting to hear from on high what I want to be when I grow up. So, Elizabeth, a smart, educated generalist with an innate sense of how to manage complex organizations, had natural appeal. And my admiration is undiminished. I believe she's a woman we can all learn a lot from, even today.

I want to spend a moment on "recognition."

One of the oblique criticisms of women's ambition is that it's selfish, self-aggrandizing, putting yourself forward in an unseemly way. At my all-girls high school, for example, if you wanted elected office the surest path to defeat was to say so. Well, I think recognition is vital to organizational success, particularly for women, and I urge you not to shy away from it. And I mean recognition on as broad a basis as possible.

When I was little and first grasped the concept of mortality, my perhaps peculiar response was that fame was the only appropriate goal. Something along the lines of "the only point of living is if someone, preferably many someones, will remember you once you're dead."

Luckily I've modified that view, but a kernel of it still remains — the need to have an impact, make a difference, make stuff happen. The recognition part — the fame — has kind of receded into the role of what Micheline Bouchard, president of Motorola Canada, described as "being visibly competent" *all the time* — and this is why it's important. The ongoing reinforcement of *being seen to be successful* helps people get over the hurdle of placing their personal eggs in a woman's basket.

Many of us have a problem seeking the limelight, particularly when it comes as a result of a group rather than personal effort. We've been socialized to not see ourselves as the centre of the universe, and we're not. But that doesn't mean we can't take a bullet for the team, does it? After all, someone has to represent them? If you accept that women are at a deficit when it comes to organizational confidence, then I think Micheline was spot on when she advised us that it's not enough to be competent, *one has to be seen to be competent* in order to get ahead. And ink, lots of ink, is a proven route to credit for competence, perhaps even more credit than one deserves!

A very good friend of mine, yes one of the Italian adventurers, once confided in me that she couldn't see herself running an organization. She claimed she saw herself much more in the role of a #2 — power behind the throne, good woman behind the man — you know the line, pretty classic limit to a woman's ambition. This woman happens to be extremely smart, enormously hard working, capable of inspiring huge degrees of confidence in colleagues, customers, and employees and yet, at the time, she didn't see herself in the #1 position.

Many men of my acquaintance, with half the natural gifts and way less experience, would absolutely envision themselves in the corner office. The difference: self-confidence. Not commitment, not balance issues, not disgust for the politics of advancement — just plain self-image. I think many women's' ambitions are at odds with their self-confidence, and because we fail to celebrate ambition in women, the self-confidence problem can overwhelm.

The good news, of course, is you can work these things out. One of the ways I've always managed the conflict between my aspirations and my self-image has been not to build the 5-year or the 10-year plan — I always found that a bit overwhelming — but to focus on the next role, my boss's job, or even my boss's boss's job. That way, I could use my natural ability to learn, to get it, to master the current challenge, to quite quickly see myself in the next role.

Self-confidence, or lack of it, didn't come into it, because I wasn't really reaching for something very far off. Well, apply that model, and pretty soon you are looking at the top job in the organization. And my friend? Happily she's since changed her tune and is now perfectly at ease with the idea of running the show, which one day soon she undoubtedly will.

I chose to speak this morning on the subject of ambition because I know it exists in all of us. Having worked with many smart, competent women and men, I am convinced that, by and large, women in organizations use their innate ambition to less advantage than their male counterparts. Whether it's because it's inherently in conflict with our feminine socialization, or because we rationalize the suppression of corporate ambition against competing interests, the fact remains that both men and women are more comfortable with ambitious *men*.

I want you to ignore this fact and:

Acknowledge and be proud of your ambition. Celebrate the fact that you want to go far! And while you're at it, celebrate it in others, especially other women.

I want you to:

Consciously reject all the baggage and barriers that have built up along the way on why things have not worked out … the biases, blame, equality, leadership issues, self-doubt, guilt, and the list goes on and on … *they block ambitions.*

I want you to:

At times be prepared to kick-start your ambition, whether you find yourself undecided on what to pursue after your first child, asking for your boss's job, whatever, but kick-starting your inner ambition will need to be done at times.

I want you to:

Set achievable, practical but not threatening goals, but do have the vision to see doing your boss's boss's job. I suspect that ambition is a lifelong gift, and so lifelong goals seem appropriate, don't you think?

I want you to:

Recognize how important it is for others to be ambitious for you. If it's you against the world, back the world! But work to imbue others with confidence for you and for themselves through you.

If you acknowledge the importance and power of your ambition, recognize that it is there to drive you to greater achievements and sustain you through the challenges, and if you couple it with competence, hard work, and the morality you learned at your mother's knee, you can defeat the insidious erosion of feeling inadequate, the fear of being in charge, the doubts that we all have about our capacity to lead.

You will be blessed with the ongoing luxury of feeling challenged but not overwhelmed, of feeling effective, competent, and like you are in fact making a difference to people. You will be gifted with the satisfaction which comes from being recognized by those whose opinion you value, as being in exactly the right place.

To end the tale of the Villa Mimosa and our unprecedented confessions on personal ambition: Within a year of that night, every single one of us had taken on a bigger, better, or at least in my case, a very different job.

Coincidence. I don't think so.

Thank you.

Book Sponsors

To our sponsors, a sincere *thank you* for investing in this book. Your continued investment in diversity and female leadership is simply remarkable. Not only were you an easy call to make, but you continue to demonstrate support throughout the project and every day in your organizations. I look forward to your use of the book in your organizations as a mentoring and storytelling asset. Together we are changing the face of corporate Canada.

Publishers Level

Microsoft Canada

RBC

TD Bank Group

Deloitte

Edelman Canada

Ogilvy

Editors Level

Blake, Cassels & Graydon LLP

Canadian Imperial Bank
  of Commerce

KPMG

Loblaw Companies Limited

McCarthy Tétrault LLP

Osler, Hoskin & Harcourt LLP

Scotiabank

Sun Life Financial

Torys LLP

With appreciation and thanks,
Colleen Moorehead

Without Whom

Collecting and assembling the many stories for this book was a challenging task. It could not have happened without the candid and enthusiastic involvement of so many touched by The Judy Project. For the selfless sharing of stories, vignettes, and lessons learned, I thank you. Our collective hope is that future female leaders can embrace their ambition, authentic voice, and "kinder, gentler" leadership attributes informed from the experience of your storytelling.

Daryl Aitken

Monique Allen

Ikram Al Mouaswas

Kimberly Armstrong

Greg Barber

Cathy Barrick

Charlotte Beers

Lorna Borenstein

Cheryl Brunato

Laura Cameron

Tiziana Casciaro

Marlene Cepparo

Rowena Chan

Cheri Chevalier

Frank Clegg

Alison Coville

Beatrix Dart

Emma Da Silva

Sarah Davis

Shauna Emerson O'Neill

Heather Fraser

Clare Gaudet

Jennifer Gillivan

Helena Gottschling

Stacey Grant-Thompson

Jhale Hajiyeva

Margaret Heffernan

Paula Hodgins

Pamela Hughes

Martine Irman

Emily Jelich

Dawn Jetten

Janet Kestin

Aileen Kheraj

Lisa Kimmel

Jane Kinney

Paula Knight	Lindsay Sacknoff
Genviève Lavertu	Sandra Sanderson
Shelly Lazarus	Tracy Sandler
Tina Lee	Kerri-Ann Santaguida
Linda MacKay	Sandy Sharman
Sharon MacLeod	Geeta Sheker
Mary Lou Maher	Colleen Sidford
Kim Mason	Andrea Stairs
Erin Mclean	Anne Sutherland
Carol McNamara	Kathleen Taylor
Sandra Palmaro	Maria Theofilaktidis
Natasha Pekelis	Bill Thomas
Simone Philogène	John Thompson
Denise Pickett	Daria Thorp
Dale Ponder	Shari Walczak
Sandra Rondzik Popik	Beth Wilson
David Powell	Pamela Winsor
Susan Ross	Annette Verschuren
Jane Russell	Nancy Vonk

Special thanks to Barlow Books publisher Sarah Scott, who added her passion to bring this book to life, along with writer Bonnie Munday, developmental editor Joanne Sutherland, and the excellent production and design team led by Tracy Bordian that included Ruth Dwight and Karen Alliston.

For all of us, this was indeed a passion project. You have my sincere thanks for getting us across the line!

With thanks,
Colleen Moorehead

Behind The Judy Project

There is a small group of individuals, the Steering Committee, who were the driving force behind the foundations of the Judy Project. I would like to recognize them for their early collective vision, unwillingness to compromise on the content, commitment to focusing on "fixing from the top," and uncompromising goal to first serve the needs of participants by acknowledging the whole female leader.

I would like to recognize Rotman's role as an ambitious and passionate partner learning institution in creating a unique, intensely experiential, exclusive forum that continues to lead the market today. The Judy Project was, and remains, a true collaboration.

Through your efforts, we have achieved the original mission statement of making our collective corporate organizations stronger today.

THE JUDY PROJECT STEERING COMMITTEE

Daryl Aitken
Janet Kestin
Paula Knight
Bukurie Kulla
Colleen Moorehead
David Powell
Cathy Preston
Janice Rubin
Anne Sutherland
Judith Wright

Frank Clegg
Lorna Borenstein

THE ROTMAN TEAM

Roger Martin
Brian Golden
Geeta Sheker
Ariana Bradford
Michael Hartmann
Alex Vaccari
Tiziana Casciaro
Beatrix Dart

The Judy Project
Sponsors

The members of The Judy Project Steering Committee, the Rotman School of Management, and the University of Toronto are grateful to the donors and sponsors who have contributed generously to this exceptional program, and for their commitment to the leadership development of program participants.

FOUNDING SPONSOR:
Microsoft Canada

SPONSORS:
AMEX Canada Inc.
Bell Canada
Bentall Capital
Best Buy Canada Ltd.
Blake, Cassels & Graydon LLP
CAE Inc.
Canada Post Corporation
Canadian Imperial Bank
  of Commerce
Canadian Marketing
  Association
CBC Television
Chubb Insurance Company
  of Canada
Corus Entertainment Inc.
Cossette Communication
  Group
Deloitte & Touche
eBay Canada Limited
E★TRADE Canada
GE Canada
Glencore (Noranda
  Falconbridge/Xstrata)
Hewlett Packard (Canada) Co.
Hudson's Bay Company
IBM
Inco Limited
Institute of Communications
  and Advertising
KPMG LLP
Loblaw Companies Limited
Maple Leaf Foods

McCarthy Tétrault LLP
Medtronic of Canada Limited
Microsoft Canada
Molson Inc.
Ontario Power Generation
Osler, Hoskin & Harcourt LLP
RBC Financial Group
Rogers
S.C. Johnson and Son Limited
Tangerine (ING Direct)
TAXI Advertising & Design
TD Bank Financial Group
TELUS Communications Inc
Women in Capital Markets

FRIENDS:

ALTANA Pharma
Bentall Capital
Cisco Systems Canada Co.
London Drugs Limited
Maclean's Magazine
Maple Leaf Sports &
  Entertainment Ltd.
National Leasing
The Kingbridge Centre

The Judy Project Distinguished Speakers

2003–2018

The Judy Project is one of Canada's leading executive forums, uniquely designed to support and prepare women who are ascending into executive leadership and C-suite positions. Employing a variety of learning approaches, the Program integrates leading academic research by Rotman School of Management Faculty with expertise from an impressive roster of distinguished CEO and Executive guest speakers from Canadian and global organizations.

Over its first 16 years, The Judy Project has been very fortunate in attracting so many leading thought leaders to share their experience and expertise with participants, among them:

Nancy Adler, S. Bronfman Chair in Management, Desautels Faculty of Management, McGill University

Elyse Allan, President and Chief Executive Officer, GE Canada

Charlotte Beers, Former Chair and Chief Executive Officer of Ogilvy & Mather Worldwide

Lorna Borenstein, Chief Executive Officer, Grokker

Elaine Campbell, President, AstraZeneca Canada Inc.

Tiziana Casciaro, Academic Co-Director, The Judy Project; Professor of Organizational Behaviour and HR Management and Jim Fisher Professor of Leadership Development, Rotman School of Management

Frank Clegg, Former President of Microsoft Canada Inc., Chief Executive Officer of Canadians for Safe Technology

Alison Coville, President, Hudson's Bay Company and Home Outfitters

Isabelle Courville, President, Hydro-Québec TransÉnergie

Christine Cushing, Celebrity TV Chef

Wendy Dobson, Professor and Co-Director for the Institute of International Business at the Rotman School of Management and former Canadian Associate Deputy Minister of Finance

Victor Dodig, President and Chief Executive Officer, CIBC Group of Companies

Amy C. Edmondson, Novartis Professor of Leadership and Management, Harvard Business School, and author of *Teaming to Innovate* and *Extreme Teaming*

Robin Ely is Diane Doerge Wilson Professor of Business Administration, Harvard Business School, and faculty chair of the HBS Gender Initiative

Jim Fisher, Professor Emeritus and former Vice-Dean and Marcel Desautels Chair in Entrepreneurship, Rotman School of Management, and author of *The Thoughtful Leader: A Model of Integrative Leadership*

Margot Franssen, Founder and Former President, The Body Shop Canada

Heather Fraser, Founder and CEO, Vuka Innovation, Inc., Adjunct Professor, Rotman School of Management, author of *Design Works: How to Tackle Your Toughest Innovation Challenges through Business Design*, and co-founder of Taxi Advertising & Design